This Last House

THIS
LAST
HOUSE
A Retirement
Memoir

Janis P. Stout

To Barbara —

Janis Stout
August 14, 2010

TCU Press
Fort Worth, Texas

Library of Congress Cataloging-in-Publication Data

Stout, Janis P.
This last house : a retirement memoir / by Janis Stout. -- 1st ed.
p. cm.
ISBN 978-0-87565-408-9 (alk. paper)
1. Stout, Janis P. 2. Stout, Janis P.--Homes and haunts. 3. Retirees--New Mexico--
Biography. 4. College teachers--Texas--Biography. 5. Home--Psychological aspects.
6. Dwellings--Psychological aspects. 7. New Mexico--Biography. 8. Texas--
Biography. I. Title.
CT275.S8755A3 2010
978.9'053092--dc22
[B]
2009033447

TCU Press
P. O. Box 298300
Fort Worth, Texas 76129
817.257.7822
http://www.prs.tcu.edu
To order books: 800.826.8911

Illustrations and design by Barbara Mathews Whitehead

Photographs courtesy of the author and are used with permission.

For my boys—

Doug

Alan

Rick

Steven

Contents

Acknowledgments

HANK YOU, Charles Rowell, for telling me, when I retired, that I ought to write a book about it. Thank you, Deborah Williams, for reading that talky first draft and saying, "It needs more story." Thank you, Trey Hammond, for reading a revised version of the first draft and finding things in it to praise; the echo of your voice saying "terrific" has kept me going. Thank you, Andrew Shimmin, for the Internet research that shored up my "I think" passages with facts. Thank you, Bonnie Shimmin, for giving the whole thing your intelligent reading and witty, right-on-target comments not once, but twice, and for reminding me that irony is OK even in a title. Thank you, Ann Pittman, for sharing your long perspective on retirement from Texas A&M University. Thank you, Judith Keeling, for being so discerning a reader, so willing to see potential, and so able to help me make a book out of it. Thank you, Judy Alter, for the intelligence and enthusiasm with which you carried me through to the end. Most of all, thank you, Loren Lutes, for living it with me; for always, ever so gently questioning me; and for sometimes leading, sometimes pushing me down the road.

INTRODUCTION

Finding Prickly Ridge

ONE JANUARY DAY in 1997 my husband and I clambered up and over a steep slope at the side of a dirt road in New Mexico and stood for the first time on the land where we would build our house for retirement.

Past the roadside embankment, the lot sloped more gradually uphill toward the back, to the crest of a ridge. It lay in that elevation band of the Sandia Mountains that means piñon and juniper trees, in addition to rocks and cactus. Lots of cactus.

We made our way cautiously up the slope to a clearing where we turned around and looked back. The realtor's car parked on a flat slab of exposed rock at the side of the road seemed far below us, and the house we had glimpsed on our way up—across the road, where the land dropped away toward the east—was now visible only as a rooftop. On beyond the drop-off, in a dusty lavender haze, lay the wide expanse of the Estancia Basin.

We knew at that moment that we had found the place we wanted to be.

It was cold and blowy with a hint of sleet in the air. Even Diane, the realtor, who was used to the climate and better dressed for it than we were, hugged herself in her parka.

"Two-and-a-half acres, you say?" Loren asked.

"Right. Two point four seven."

That was a little smaller than we had thought we were looking for. (We were then entertaining a fantasy of keeping goats.) Even so, we both knew this two-and-a-half-acre site was what we wanted. We

Our land in New Mexico as it looked before we built on it.

looked at each other and lifted our eyebrows. Loren's face bore a look of elation.

"We'll call you when we get back to Texas," he said. That was so we could talk before making an offer. But on the plane that afternoon, all the way back, I kept worrying that somebody else would buy it before we could get to the phone.

For more than a year, we had been talking about where to retire. University professors, both of us, we liked to believe we took a logical approach to things. So instead of starting by thinking of places we might like to go, we had first defined our criteria, and only then made a list of possibilities—some of which actually met the criteria. Then we gradually narrowed it down. All that time, we had avoided the *when* question, and in fact still didn't know the answer to that one. But now we at least knew *where*.

It would be another five years before we actually walked out of our offices for the last time, to go build our house. During those five years we spent untold hours planning. We leafed through magazines and books of house plans, looking for the right one. At first these were plans for log homes, because Loren thought that was what he wanted. But then I persuaded him to move on to more conventional houses, and we pored over those. We browsed in home stores, considering cabinets, sinks, hardware, floor tile—all those things that go into building a house. Finally we ordered a set of plans to use as a starting point, and Loren painstakingly drew the layout into his computer so it could be altered. Over and over we changed it, compulsively. He even built a little model of the house so we could look in the windows, check out different slopes of roof, try to spot deficiencies. He built it out of thin white sheets of Styrofoam. It was so fragile we hid it in the attic when grandchildren were coming.

I'm sure the house planning process is never easy. But the stakes seemed especially high as we planned this house, precisely because it was to be our home for retirement, for the duration. This was going to be our last house. So it seemed important to get it right.

What "getting it right" meant, though, was far from obvious, since we weren't sure what retirement would be like. But the habits and interests of a lifetime gave us clues. We knew that we would want to enjoy the outdoors, and quiet, and birds. We knew we would want to continue our scholarly work, research and writing. Robert Raines asks, in his book of poems *Living the Questions*, "Who am I when I'm not working?" It's a serious question, a very serious question, and we wanted to learn the answer to it. But in our case it was also, in a sense, an irrelevant question. We wanted to keep on working, just not in the office hours, paycheck kind of way. Planning well for our house, we thought, would go far toward making both of those goals possible: both the discovery of who we would be as people who no longer had jobs to go to and the continuation of aspects of our work that we enjoyed.

We knew how very privileged we were in being able to go at it this way. Many people have no options at all when it comes to retirement. Either they have to retire before they're ready—for reasons of health or because of employer cutbacks—or they can't fully retire at all, but have to stand on their feet all day in low-paying jobs at Walmart to bridge the gap between their Social Security check and an income they can live on. Because our jobs had provided us good retirement plans to supplement Social Security, we did have options. We could choose both the *when* and the *where*, and even plan a house.

Not that we wanted anything lavish. We didn't want to impress anyone; we didn't want a house that would signify "moving up"; just a house for retirement, a retirement home that in our own minds, at least, would be nice but not fancy, roomy but not too big, comfortable and quiet. And that's what it has been. We succeeded. So this story has (so far) a happy ending, though not the ending we expected.

Houses are important in many ways—for security and for comfort, yes, but also as expressions of who we are and what we value. But I think they not only reflect who we are, they *shape* who we are, both in childhood and later on. So they are well worth thinking about.

As soon as we think the word "house," associations dart through our mind's eye, like rabbits leaping down a path. "House," we think, and we see maybe a child's crayon drawing of a square box with a triangle on top for a roof, a spiral of smoke coming from a chimney, a door smack in the middle with a window on each side, a scribble of green grass, and probably two flowers. Where do those pictures come from? Probably not two in a hundred kids live in houses that look remotely like that. Yet that is what they draw. And those cozy images from far back in childhood come trailing into our minds when we think "house" even more readily than the kinds of images builders and realtors plant before our eyes in the Sunday papers. The reason, of course, is that this childhood image is so deeply rooted and avoids so many complications that real houses in the real marketplace entail, especially in these troubled times of foreclosures and upside-down mortgages.

I once read somewhere that the novelist Anne Tyler, when asked what her favorite book had been as a child, named *The Little House*, by Virginia Lee Burton. I was curious why she had chosen that particular book, so I went to the library and found it. It's a picture book with simple text. And in both pictures and story-line the center of everything is a little house looking quite a bit like those standard pictures children draw. Changes flow past the little house as the years go on, and once the house even gets loaded onto a truck and moved, but always it remains the focal point. With that as her favorite childhood book, is it any wonder that Tyler writes the novels she does, full of people always wanting to leave home and then always wanting to come back?

Anne Tyler is only a few years younger than I am. We are both members of what has been, I think, a peculiarly house-minded generation. Sometimes I feel like a character invented by Anne Tyler—wanting to be on the move yet wanting even more to stay at home, never able to reconcile the two.

I have lived in a great many houses. Former President Jimmy Carter states in *The Virtues of Aging* that his and Rosalynn's home in Plains, Georgia, is their sixteenth place of residence. Well, I've lived in more than that. And it seems to me that there is a certain adventure in moving around a lot. It gives us a chance to experience different places and different ways of living. It broadens one's outlook. But it also has its downsides. In my own life, these have included escalating debt, false values, and worst of all, my sons' having arrived at their own maturity with no sense of a stable home place. These were downsides of which I had only the merest inkling at the time I was engaging in what Sharon O'Brien calls, in *The Family Silver*, a kind of great American house-swap. I was as caught up in the mentality of sequential occupying as anyone else.

That is, in my first marriage. In my second, a second marriage for both of us, Loren and I didn't move nearly so much during our working years, and never for reasons of corporate transfer or trading up. Still, we did live in several different places before we retired, and when we add together the moves we made as a couple and all the ones we had made before, we see that it was quite a trail that led us to that cold, prickly ridge in New Mexico.

Sometimes I picture my whole life as a long row of houses. There I am, emerging from the first, going in the door of the next, then out again and into the next, and so on down the row. They are different houses, and I am myself a little different each time. They, and the life I lived within their walls, shaped who I became as I prepared to move into this last house, the house of retirement. I can't write about the choosing of this place and the planning of our retirement house without thinking through the sequence of all the houses that came before it. And I can't write about retirement without thinking about my work life and what my career, the mere fact of having a career at all, meant to me. They are all bound up together.

PART ONE

Remembrance of Houses Past

The house on Richardson Street at its best.

CHAPTER ONE

The Rock House on Richardson Street

ORANGE-BROWN rock walls. Steep gables. Sometimes green, sometimes brown wood trim. This is the house of my Fort Worth childhood, where I first opened my eyes on the world. This was the start of the trail that would finally lead to the mountains of New Mexico and our retirement home.

The rock house on Richardson had been built some time in the thirties by Dad's father and one of my uncles. I believe they built it to sell, and Mother and Dad decided to buy it. House and lot together, in those Great Depression days, they paid the grand sum of $2,100. I heard them say it many times, always in tones of amazement: twenty-one hundred dollars, house and lot.

The house was small even for just the three of us—two bedrooms, one bath, a tiny kitchen—and truly cramped when my maternal grandmother, Granny, periodically came to live with us. Nevertheless, it was quite simply my standard for what a house should be. Wisps of a wish to live in one of those white or pastel houses in my Dick and Jane readers might drift through my head, but when I had a grip on things I knew that the small wooden boxes that lined the rest of our street were quite inferior to our solid rock one.

It always seemed to me a very special thing to live in a house built by my own grandfather, especially since I never knew him. He died a week before I was born. My other grandfather had died long years before, when Mother was only two. So I had no grandfather at all, and I always envied children who did. I often rummaged through the picture box in the floor of the hall closet to gaze at a blurry snapshot taken of me at maybe a month old. This was in 1939, before the start of the war in Europe. I am lying on some kind of flowered cloth spread on the grass, with the irregular rock of the house in the background, the rock that my grandfather, Jake Pitts, had put up and mortared in. I didn't have him, but I had his house.

My very earliest memory is this: I am standing pressed against my mother's legs on the back steps of the house. She is holding a flashlight. Its circle of illumination spills onto the brown rock, but its center is trained on my father's gloved hands, grasping and lifting a dog—a dog caught by the neck between the pickets of our gate! A naturally fearful man, he is maneuvering gingerly to avoid being bitten, but is making himself do what he has to do. He lifts the dog to where the pickets taper diagonally into points so it can breathe, and then on higher until he has it free. Two days short of my second birthday (I know this from hearing them say, many times, that the dog incident happened the night before my tonsils were removed, and my tonsils were removed the day before I turned two), I am not so much scared as I watch this as I am excited and determined to see what is going on.

Later, when I said something about the dog trapped by its neck in the gate pickets, they thought I only remembered hearing about it, but it was very clear to me, a strong visual memory, and it still is.

It seems there was an old man who would drive down our graveled street about dusk in a wagon pulled by a pair of mules, and this greyhound of his would run along off to the side, cutting across backyards and jumping fences. Why, I can't even begin to think—either why the old man drove through or why the dog chose not to stay alongside the wagon in the street or else ride. This particular time, it was unlucky enough to try to jump right where the peak of our gate came up high above the rest of the fence, and failed to clear the point.

Another story from my earliest years also involves watching. Uncle Ted, the uncle who had helped build our house, come to repaper the back bedroom. I watched by the hour as he stripped off the old wallpaper with a kind of square-ended spatula before putting up the new. At some point in the process I found an opportunity to take up the stripping tool myself, and set to work. When Uncle Ted came back and found me, I had ripped off a nice little piece—a strip of the new paper he had just put up. In this case, I may only be remembering what I was told later, but there is a kind of aura of it hanging around my peripheral mental vision. In any event, I can well imagine how utterly cute they thought it was; I was a very doted-upon child.

There is no doubt, though, that I can clearly see, even now, that fiercely floral wallpaper he was hanging. I remember how its red and yellow clusters surged and wavered at me through a high fever when I had the measles.

I remember, too, the fine blue spruce by the front corner of the house that Dad cut down and brought in for our Christmas tree one year. I don't know if that was the Christmas Granny had pneumonia and couldn't come to the living room for the opening of presents. I slipped a special box out from under the tree and took it to her to open first, because I knew it was house-slippers and I reasoned that if she put them on, she would be warm enough to get up and come join us. And of course she did.

And then there was the Christmas when my other grandmother, the one I called Mema, an eccentric woman if not actually crazy, insisted we line up in the short little hall and march into the living room to the tree singing "Onward Christian Soldiers." And we did— to Mother's great displeasure. As Theodore Roethke writes in one of his poems, her face "could not unfrown itself."

In a Gingerbread House in the War Years

My memories circle back and back. One moment I see myself at age four, pestering some of the few visitors we ever had. I'm parading into the living room with my cousin Barbara; we're announcing "blackout!" and turning off the lights. Nobody seems amused. Next I see myself at age seven, sprawled in an upholstered rocking chair in my parents' bedroom, reading. There, not in the living room, because we did not engage in recreational sitting in the living room; it was kept nice for company. And I liked that bedroom chair because if I took a break from reading I could dangle my head over its upholstered arm to look down the hall upside-down and imagine a house in which I would have to step over those pieces of wall above the doors to get from room to room. Now I'm four again and starting to take piano lessons from my cousin Bonnie, the daughter of my Aunt Clemmie. An excellent pupil, I reach the third grade book by the time I'm five. Mother and Dad are very proud. Then one day when we arrive for my lesson I am unable to play a single note. I sit on the bench and can't, or won't, so much as touch the keys. It's as if my body itself were rebelling. I remember how traumatic it was for everyone. They had been so proud, they had so liked it that I was exceptional, a prodigy, and I had let them down. After a year, when I started taking lessons again, I had to begin at the beginning.

But there had already been another trauma during that year of piano lessons with Bonnie: the day I got stuck to a pole. I was still four, and Mother and I were waiting for the bus, going to my lesson. It was raining, and we took refuge under the leaky canopy of an abandoned gas station. Idly, I took hold of one of the poles holding up the canopy and couldn't let go. Mother was screaming and trying to pull me off, but I was stuck, held fast by an electric current running through it. Somehow, in my struggling and pulling, I managed to get my mouth stuck too! Fortunately, a passerby jumped out of his car and knocked me off the pole with a blow. We went on to my lesson.

When I lolled in the platform rocker in the back bedroom doing whatever I was doing, Mother was always just a few steps away in the kitchen, or running the vacuum, or going in and out drying clothes on the line. That is, she was always working while I read or embroidered or played paper dolls or daydreamed, there in that house with its orange-brown rock exterior and its exaggerated gables, its shortage of space and its abundance of wallpaper.

Proud as I was of our rock-solid house, and certain as I was that it was the best house on the block, I'm sure I was not nearly as proud as my mother. I didn't understand at the time, of course, but only much later, what it must have meant to her. She had been born and raised on a poor dirt farm in East Texas. There were eight of them, the last one born fatherless, and Granny had kept them alive working the farm herself, plowing and picking the cotton and taking it to Clarksville to sell, chopping the wood, milking, raising a garden, with only what help the children could give as they grew up. Some time in the late twenties she rented the farm to a son-in-law and moved to Fort Worth at the urging of some of the other older ones who'd already gone. Mother was in her mid-teens at the time. She got a job at Woolworth's and ruined her feet standing on a concrete floor behind a counter, envying girls who had good clothes and prospects. She would never get over her self-consciousness of her country origins and her seventh-grade education, just as Granny would never get over wishing to be back where she came from.

No wonder the house meant so much to her—or that her family considered her uppity! No wonder she was so determined to dress me better than any other girl in class when I started school! And with a rock house and all my starched dresses in the closet and all my straight-A report cards, I suppose it's no wonder I felt that I was better. Only once did I ever feel less than queen in my little world. A neighbor kid asked me, in a mocking tone, why my father went to work at night instead of in the morning. I said that Dad was a musician and was playing jobs (he never said "gigs"). But the boy wouldn't believe me. He said Daddy was a burglar. I was mortified. I know now that the only thing we were at the top of was a distinctly lower middle class. Even then I knew there were fancier neighborhoods across town; I had seen those stately houses when we went to the zoo. But they were a different world. What mattered was my world, my house.

I became vaguely aware, though, that it was just slightly peculiar. The front door opened from an enclosed porch, rock-floored and rock-walled, with an arched opening toward the street through which the postman and the Watkins Products salesman came up the flagstone walk and two stone steps to the door. A second arch, facing toward the driveway side, served no purpose at all except to let in a little light and provide me a place to jump off the porch to the shady ground below, where a tall shrub of some kind screened the living room window. At the other front corner, by my bedroom, where a strip of roof continued down past the rock side wall, there was a third arch even more useless than the second. This one opened onto an empty rock-paved terrace with a rose garden behind it more visible to the neighbors than to us. With all these arches and the sharply peaked gables and the brown color of the rock, the house looked like one that Hansel and Gretel might have stumbled on, deep in the Black Forest.

The gables were a major challenge for Dad. Always conscientious about home maintenance, he liked to scrape and repaint the wood trim on a regular schedule, but he was too afraid of heights to do the peaks of the gables. So at least once—I think this must have been shortly after the war when Uncle Ted and Uncle Pon had just come home and were casting about for something to do—he hired one or the other of them to do the high parts. I gasped to see this daring uncle of mine, perched high above the rose garden and the never-used terrace, walk the ladder to the next section to be painted rather than climb down to move it. Probably it was Uncle Pon, the daredevil of the family, whose odd nickname came from his having begged Mema for bread, *pan,* in the largely Spanish-speaking town of San Simon, Arizona, where he and Daddy were born. A snapshot taken in the South Pacific, where he served in the Seabees, shows a cocky look. He died by suicide before the forties were out. I remember Daddy standing in the backyard alone after he and Mother came back from the funeral.

Our living room was just large enough to hold, at close quarters, a small sofa, two or maybe three upholstered chairs, and a spinet piano. Except for the hours I spent practicing there, it was never used. When I think about that forbidden room, I have a visual impression of striped wallpaper in a maroon sort of color and a small gas stove in the never-used fireplace, flanked by a pair of little tables that my mother called (to my unfailing amusement) commodes. They were quite attractive little tables, dark, with an open space above a shallow drawer and tapered legs that curved outward, ending in brass tips. I wonder what became of them. Each had its own flower-shaped ashtray, one blue, one pink, and there was a small, ornately carved coffee table with inlay top in front of the sofa. At Christmas the tree was crowded in somehow, and there was hard, colorful ribbon candy in a glass bowl.

The front bedroom, which Granny and I shared when she was with us, was wallpapered in blue with yellow flowers. It had a heater like the one in the living room that was rarely lit, Mother being worried about gas leaks. But it wasn't really needed anyway, because very little ever went on in that bedroom except when, on rare occasions, Mother decided to do her ironing there. She always kept the radio on while she ironed, and I sat on the floor and listened along with her to *Lorenzo Jones* and *Backstage Wife,* those fifteen-minute soaps of the day. Granny always wanted to raise the shade and sit by the front window to watch the world go by—not

Granny, in the backyard of the house where I began.

that much of it ever did—but Mother didn't approve. She called it "tacky."

Every time, Granny would look amazed. "What's tacky about it?"

"It's just so country. You don't sit at the window and wave at people in town."

"If the shade was up, I could just look out through the curtains."

"Oh, Mama, you'd be handling them, of course, and get them all limp."

The curtains always put an end to it. They were criss-crossed ruffled organdy, stiffly starched and a day-long job to iron. But when Granny got her little apartment on Avenue G, there were always two straight chairs by the window, with her radio on a little rickety table nearby, and in the daytime the curtains were pushed back for unobstructed watching of the sidewalk and the nearby traffic on Vaughn Boulevard.

Mother and Dad's bedroom, at the other end of the hall, was Activity Central. It was there that I got dressed on winter mornings after I started to school, sitting on the scratchy wool rug by the gas heater beside their closet door, in a half-circle of light and warmth. And there that I did my cutting out of paper dolls and coloring in coloring books, sitting on a patch of bare floor in the doorway where I could overhear Mother and Granny's kitchen talk. And of course there, in their bed, that I spent my days whenever I had to stay home from school with a fever. I was a sickly child.

One of those times, Uncle Buel came to keep me company. (Mother's brothers and sisters all had these odd names; hers was Helean, pronounced Hee-lun.) It seems wildly improbable that he would do so, because the two families did not visit back and forth or call on each other for favors, yet there he was, I'm sure of it. I must have been about nine or ten, because that was the year Mother went to work in a department store, which explains why I was home alone. I had a big ugly tomcat at the time with the incongruous name of Dolly—I had mistakenly thought he was a girl. Dolly started yowling, and Uncle Buel said the cat must need to go out and he would go open the door. But I absolutely had a fit, insisting that the cat did not need to go and I did not want him let outside. So, as usual, I got my way, and sure enough, Dolly went and pooped behind the blonde buffet in the dining room. "See?" he said. "Told you so." One end of the buffet was left standing out away from the wall for a day or so after Mother cleaned up the mess that night.

The blonde oak buffet, table, and chairs in our little dining room, just behind the sacrosanct living room, were a tight squeeze. But then, everything was a tight squeeze in that house. The buffet had a spare compartment, though, where Daddy kept a few books. Among them was a volume of Edgar Allan Poe stories. I could scare myself witless any day of the week with its horrific black-and-white illustrations. He also owned, for reasons I can't fathom, a copy of *The World of Washington Irving,* by Van Wyck Brooks—my first exposure to literary criticism. Then there were a number of little flimsy paper booklets, parts of some long-ago subscription series. One had a story involving a great many large spiders that I could never make myself read clear through. Another was about the mathematics of squaring the circle. Dad always had a curiosity about odd bits of lore.

The tiny kitchen, on the back of the house, had crudely built white cabinets—the mark of my grandfather's low standards for interior finishing—along one short wall with the refrigerator facing them in isolation on the opposite wall, and a gas range at the end. I can remember standing on a chair at the counter, watching Mama stir Jell-O®, and how the grayish film on top went around and around in slow whirls until it disappeared into the bright pink. I also liked watching her stir orange powder into the white margarine we got during the war years, to turn it butter-yellow. Another kitchen pastime when I was very small was sitting in the bottom drawer of the range where pans were kept. I always felt just a slight frisson lest the flames of the oven suddenly ignite. Apparently I was not only a sickly child but also one given to worrying. And I did get hurt in the kitchen once, though not by the gas flame. As they told it, I was two and was jitterbugging on the freshly waxed floor and fell, cutting the point of my chin clear through to the bone. They always insisted that I never struggled or even cried while old Dr. Terrell stitched it up. The scar has receded and is now tucked inconspicuously under my chin.

But perhaps the most vivid of all kitchen memories from those early years was one that involved the really nice thick wooden drainboard that Daddy kept shiny and sound by periodically resealing it with a coat of what he called Marine Spar. I liked the sound of it— "marine spar"—and have believed ever since that it must be one of the world's greatest products. But that didn't matter when one day Mother picked me up, sat me on the drainboard, and told me to open my mouth wide while she brandished a butcher knife and said she was going to cut out my tongue. It seems I was sticking it out at people, and she had decided to put a stop to it. I fully believed she was going to cut it out, and promised most fervently never to stick out my tongue at anyone ever again.

THE GREEN CAVE

When I was twelve and my brother was born, Mother and Dad decided we simply had to have more space. Instead of moving to another house, they remodeled. Daddy got Uncle Ted to help him draw up some plans and hired a carpenter. Of course, they never even considered moving out while the work was done; that would have cost way too much. So for endless months we lived in the mess, often with no functioning kitchen, sometimes with no functioning bathroom, and with a baby in the house.

The great remodeling more than doubled the size of the house. The entire living room-dining room-kitchen side became one long living-dining room; the bedrooms and bath stayed as they were; and a large addition was put on the back with another bath and walk-in closet, a big square family room, and a large eat-in kitchen. Why no third bedroom, I don't know. They must have thought it would run the cost up just too much. Good stonemasons no longer being readily available in the family, the new part was sided with wood and painted brown, to try to make it blend in. The rock house was now a half-rock house.

Inside, all the walls were Sheetrocked, and the new combination living-dining room was painted a pungent olive green—except for a strip of wallpaper above a chair-rail at the dining room end. Ceiling and all, dark olive green. The old man doing the work tried to tell Mother the ceiling ought to be white, but no, she had seen a picture in a magazine of an allover green room and that was what she wanted. Big mistake. With only the same dinky windows as before, and with matching green draperies covering them, it was a dark and gloomy room. We referred to it as "the green cave." I'm sure my insistence on white ceilings and many windows in my own later houses sprang from that too-green, too-dark room that was supposed to have been so beautiful.

I continued to practice piano for an hour or two a day in the living room, but otherwise, with its two new velvet chairs and new mahogany dining room furniture at the end, it was basically devoted to being saved, just as before. Even the shades of the two new lamps were kept in the cellophane wrapping they had come in to preserve them from dust.

The two bedrooms were also Sheetrocked and painted, the front one a strong blue and the back one, still Mother and Dad's room but also the baby's now, a choking dusty rose—again, ceiling and all.

The big new kitchen had an abundance of gleaming white steel cabinets, making up for the shortage of cabinets Mother had endured all those years. She chose red rubber tile for the floor, and bright red wallpaper with a design of green leafy latticework for the walls and, you guessed it, ceiling. It was the reddest kitchen you ever saw.

Poor Mother, she so wanted a nice house, but even after all that work, the house on Richardson Street just never was.

MARKING TIME

Just as houses are markers of people's finances or social class, they are also markers of how we define our selves. And certainly, as we look back, they are keys to unlocking our memories of the selves from which we grew up and emerged.

As I look back at the house where I began, and remember again my pride in it and how I came to understand that not everyone would have felt such pride, I recognize too that I felt a certain inevitability about it, as if I, myself, could not have existed anywhere else. I was defined by its hard rock walls: rigid, inclined to be priggish, inclined to close myself off. When a girl my age told me a nasty little joke one Saturday when I was visiting Granny, I informed her she wasn't nice and refused to play with her ever again. Granny scolded me. She thought it was because the girl was homely, or because she had to do chores instead of play all the time, or because she didn't have a nice house. That wasn't it at all, but I never explained and never relented.

My mother catered to me and bragged about me and bought me clothes, but also, I knew, expected me not to assert my will against hers in any way. So I played the role of the good little girl, careful not to slip up. After all, I was the child who, at three, had been threatened with having her tongue cut out and at four had gotten her tongue and hands stuck to a metal pipe with an electrical current in it. Is it any wonder that the first time I ever truly shocked her was by saying damn? Not that it was the only time I shocked her; there were others. By high school I knew that my perfection in playing the good girl role was choking me. I had felt the tension of her expectations too long. I had to break out if I was going to breathe.

I had been raised in the fifties way. Whether anyone ever actually said it I'm not sure, but I had absorbed, as if from the very air around me, the idea that I could be a teacher or a nurse or a secretary, nothing else. Actually, as valedictorian of my class I could have had many prospects, but my horizons were limited to those few. So teacher it was; I would teach English in high school. As for choosing a college, I had no idea what I was doing, no understanding at all that one might be better than another. But one of my friends was going to

Texas Tech, out in Lubbock, so I decided to go along. Supposedly there were four boys to every girl. But I never found out, because I never went.

The Saturday afternoon before graduation, I was sitting on the porch of our neighbor's house spouting off about my plans—how I would go to college and room with my friend, then get a teaching job and my own apartment.

"I can't believe this!" she broke in. "I can't believe you would think of living away from home, not married!"

It came over me like a big wave: I was never going to get away. I said those very words to myself, silently, in my mind: I'm never going to get away.

That very month, at my summer job, I met a guy just out of the army who was going back to finish his degree at North Texas, in Denton. We became engaged, I switched to North Texas at the last minute, and in October, barely into my freshman year, we were married. If only I had waited even two or three months, college itself would have given me the escape I needed. Instead, I married at seventeen, mainly, I think now, to get away from my mother.

As I look back, I can see that she was depressed. Her perfectionist housekeeping was a way of establishing a sense of self-worth. Soon after the remodeling was finished, Mother had to have a hysterectomy, and my wild and crazy favorite aunt, Aunt Ruby, came from the far-off Texas Panhandle to help out. I was assigned the care of baby Kenny, and she and Granny were to do the cooking and cleaning. Mother had made it clear that the new flagstone patterned family room floor was to be mopped on some regular schedule—maybe once a week, maybe every other day, whatever. So Aunt Ruby mopped according to the schedule. But she wasn't careful to avoid splashing soapy water onto the wooden quarter-round along the paneled walls, and I guess Mother said something about it. Maybe this wasn't her only inadequacy in housekeeping that was pointed out. In any event, Aunt Ruby went home in a huff.

Mother, a perfectionist in dress as well as in housekeeping.

Even then, as a youngster of thirteen, I wondered how much harm her mopping was going to do in the few short weeks she would be there and how that slight risk could possibly be worth making a point over. It occurred to me that this was giving a house—the physical fact of a house—more importance than it merited. Yes, it's good to take care of things. But to worry about getting the quarter-round wet and create a grudge between sisters over it! Maybe a good answer would have been not to mop so often.

But there was more. In the same way that her housekeeping was a way of constructing a sense of self-worth, her perfectionist demands on me were a way of reliving and reconstructing her own unsatisfactory life. As Jung writes, "The greatest burden on the child is the unlived life of the parent."

A few months after I married, I saw her fly into a rage and slap my five-year-old brother across the face for a trifling cause—saw it for the first and only time, though he tells me now that it happened a lot, and he was afraid of her. When I saw that, I knew there was rage inside her. I didn't know why and still don't—partly, I'm sure, because any glitches in the perfection of her efforts to fulfill her life through mine were deadly threatening to her. She must have been, all those years, always at the breaking point in her effort to get it right. That would account for the time she switched my legs until they bled because I had misbehaved and embarrassed her in front of one of her friends. It all fits. And by marrying so early, I had violated her greatest taboo of all: sex.

But now, as I write this, I wonder if there was something more, something hidden, a deeper source of her rage. When she was growing up, down in East Texas on a little subsistence farm, she had wanted desperately to keep going to school beyond the seventh grade, the last grade offered at the only nearby school—wanted it desperately enough to repeat that grade rather than accept quitting. But then her oldest sister's husband started driving an early morning milk route into the nearest town, and she could ride with him. I wonder about those rides before daylight. She was very intense about it when she told me once about that year she tried to go to high school. They got to town so early, she said, that the school wasn't open yet, and she had nowhere to go. So when winter came, and it was cold, she quit. A girl that desperate to go to school quit rather than ride in on a wagon, in the early morning dark, with her brother-in-law. That would account, wouldn't it, for the submerged rage and the antipathy to sex? And it would also account for her determination to re-live her life through me?

That wish—quite openly expressed—to take over my life in order to fulfill her own drove me out the door even more than the simmering rage that lifted her hand to slap a five-year-old, hard, for nothing more than asking when she would bring his piece of chicken for his dinner plate. A good looking, personable guy came along who was after me, and I went.

The house built of orange-brown rock, which became half rock and half wood siding, was where I lived until I graduated from high school at seventeen, started to college, and a month later, married. Mother and Dad never had to face the question of whether to move my brother into my old bedroom because they moved away also. The property on Richardson Street had been bought by the city to make room for a new freeway, and the house itself was sold at auction. But when the house movers took off the rock siding from the old part and hoisted it onto their rig, the house my grandfather had built broke in two at the seam where the addition had been put on. They set the two pieces on a foundation a couple of blocks away. Whoever it was that had bought it patched it up, but never bothered to put the rock back on. Years later, I drove by. It had a very sad look about it.

CHAPTER TWO

All Those Way Stations

*W*HEN I MARRIED Glenn—that's what I'll call him —I entered a life of perpetual moving. Partly, this was because of his enormous restlessness, but also it was just the way things were then. We were a mobile generation. But we were also a house-minded one. Trading up was the paradigm of the day. Our minds weren't on being at home and making a life as much as they were on getting a better house—which meant a bigger, more expensive house. I don't think we ever envisioned world peace as fervently as we envisioned separate dining rooms and wallpaper accents.

If my count is correct, Glenn and I lived in eighteen different places in our twenty-four and three-quarters years together. Memories cluster around them all as I count through them, one by one—way stations along the trail of my struggle to become a person.

THE FIRST FOUR APARTMENTS PLUS ONE

After the wedding we went home to (#1) a garage apartment on Sycamore Street in Denton, near the campus of what was then North Texas State University. I was a freshman, Glenn a junior, and we had almost no money, so we had been relieved to find a place for forty dollars a month, furnished. I described it to Mother as "cute," but it was actually pretty grim. Up tottery stairs over a garage behind the owner's house, it was a faded, tattered, faintly grimy kind of place with window shades discolored to a crisp brown and peeling linoleum floors that billowed in windy weather. But even if it had been cute, I wouldn't have known how to keep it. A pampered child who'd never done chores, how would I? My theory of taking out garbage was, ignore it and maybe it'll go away. My theory of cooking was, open a recipe book and wait for magic.

My dismay in the months we lived there was partly, then, at my own incompetence. But it was also at the kind of life I found myself living. Glenn's temper blow-ups—yelling, name-calling, hostile body postures, clenched fists—began the first week. I knew I could probably get an annulment, considering my age, but it would have been so embarrassing to admit to parents, teachers, all those people who had sent wedding gifts, what a mistake I'd made. People had always seemed to think I knew what I was doing. What if they thought I didn't have a clue? I couldn't bear that.

The next spring we moved to apartment #2, newly remodeled in a nice old two-story house. The rent was a little scary at sixty-five dollars, but this place really was cute—sleek and imaginative with tweed carpet and accent walls painted zingy colors and a sort of built-in dining table with bookshelf ends, neat as a pin. It also had a brand-new electric range and an air conditioner: my first experience of either. I don't know if I ever again, in all the years of that marriage, felt quite so good about a place as I did this apartment. It distracted me from all the things I didn't know how to handle. Also, it allowed me to retreat into my music. Mother and Dad bought me a piano— not the best thing for a young couple to have to move around, but very good for keeping me reminded of who I was.

In January of 1958 Glenn graduated, and I dropped out of school. B.B.A. in hand, he took a job as manager trainee with Foley's Department Store in downtown Houston, and we moved to (#3) a garden apartment in the Montrose section. Now a center of the arts community and gay life, Montrose was then just a tree-shaded neighborhood with stately older homes and a thick tree canopy. Only thing was, swarms of enormous roaches lived in those trees—a lesson, I suppose, in taking the bad with the good.

I had vague thoughts of going back to college some day, but the goal right then was to make money and save up for a house, so I got an office job downtown. On Sundays we drove around and looked at houses. It was a common recreational pastime of the day. Oh, how we wanted to buy a house! Instead, we bought our first new car. Cars and houses: the magnet poles of existence in those years.

Glenn quickly became dissatisfied with retailing. We went back to Fort Worth and moved into the front bedroom of the rock house on Richardson Street (#4) while he looked for something else. It was while we were there that I developed morning sickness.

He soon got a job with an oil company—I mean, how much better could it get? And we moved into (#5) a two-bedroom duplex in a low-rent complex that looked like barracks. The shabby bathroom and kitchen reminded me of our first apartment, and though the large pantry would have been nice if someone had scrubbed it out, no one ever did. The neighbors on the other side of the unit had loud, frequent arguments which I found interesting in that they were two-way, she gave as good as she took. But it was not an example I could follow; my style was more resentful silence. Like us, the neighbors spent their weekends looking at houses, though in a higher price range than ours. Their expectations were higher. After one Sunday's excursion she reported in shocked tones that one model home they had looked at didn't even have a fireplace! I suppose it was more or less the equivalent of being shown a house without granite countertops today.

THE FIRST HOUSE

We were determined to get into a house of our own before the baby came, and we did: a modest three-bedroom (#6) with carport, no fireplace, for $10,500. I sewed café curtains for the bedrooms and half-bath and planted periwinkles from Glenn's sister's yard along the side of the carport. Nothing I have ever planted has grown so luxuriantly as those periwinkles. The irony is clear to me now. I was working at fixing up the place and the flowers grew almost uncontrollably, but my marriage was falling apart and wilting away.

His sister had warned me not to marry him. It was good advice. He never once hit me—I want to make that clear—but he towered over me, and when he jerked my head back by the hair and yelled in my face, or when he grabbed me up by the arm, it was scary. So life in that starter home was troubled, at best. But when the baby came, our world truly caved in.

Doug was born with hydrocephalus, commonly called water on the brain. At first I didn't know what was wrong, only that it was something bad and no one would tell me. They kept him away in the nursery, and when I had a tantrum and demanded to hold my baby they said "tomorrow."

Instead, tomorrow brought the pediatrician. Dr. Terrell—Dr. Blanche, as I was used to calling her—had been my own pediatrician during most of my childhood; her much older husband, also a pediatrician, had welcomed me into the world at this very hospital, and she had taken over the practice when he retired. We were very close.

"Everyone knows birth is hard on mothers," she began, "but people don't stop to think that it's also hard on babies. Sometimes it leaves them irritable and uncomfortable. This was hard, and we're giving him sedation—" She gathered up her charts and notebooks and rushed out of the room in tears.

They gave me something to help me sleep.

When Dr. Blanche came again the next day, she brought the baby to the room with her and gave him to me to hold while she told me what was wrong. She had known, she said, as soon as she saw him, from his enlarged head and bulging fontanelle, or soft spot. She had done a tap with a needle and drawn off a huge amount of fluid. Most babies with hydrocephalus, she pointed out, also have spina bifida. Doug did not. So in that respect we were lucky. He would have the use of his legs.

I had seen a baby with hydrocephalus once when I was a child. Mother had taken me to visit someone and there was a baby. Its huge head filled half the width of the playpen where it lay and moaned. Mother kept trying to stop me from staring, but I couldn't help it. How was that baby ever going to be able to hold up such a head? Now the image rushed back, and I asked Dr. Blanche if my baby would be like that one. She assured me he would not. "There's surgery we can do now. If he lives at all, he won't be like that."

She couldn't really have known, of course, but I held onto her words during the next weeks and months as surgery followed surgery.

The first was when he was twelve days old. A neurosurgeon placed a shunt in the brain, draining into the jugular. But the shunt kept stopping up. We would take him home, and he would seem to be doing well for a few days or even a few weeks, and then he would start crying all the time and his eyes would roll back in his head and we would know the pressure was back. And then they would go in again to flush out the shunt and replace it. Once they had to re-work it before the stitches from the previous time had even been removed. There was no way we could pay the soaring bills, of course. So I found a job and left him with Mother during the day. Our new little house meant nothing to us then but a place to rush out of in the morning and back into in the evening after work, except when we were rushing out to the hospital.

THE FIRST TRANSFER

When Glenn went to work for the oil company there in Fort Worth, they had made a big point of telling him that no one had been transferred away in years—within modern memory. Before Doug was a year old, word came that the office was being closed. Glenn was one of the lucky ones who would still have a job—in Houston. Back we went.

He went ahead to scout out the new house market, but everything seemed too expensive, so we rented (#7) a three bedroom with

*Summer 1960, with Doug, in the backyard of our first house,
way station number six.*

cedar-shake siding across the street from Bellaire High School.
Probably the nicest thing about it was the luxuriant stand of St.
Augustine grass in its shady yard and the geraniums along the back
fence. Less nice was the matted cotton carpeting that shed so copi-
ously you'd have thought it would long ago have shed itself away to
nothing. Doug was finally starting to crawl, and his corduroy overalls
acted like one of those rollers you use to pick up lint off your suit.
Five minutes on the floor and he was a puffball.

I had turned twenty-one in May, so that November I was old
enough to vote for the first time. It was 1960, the Kennedy-Nixon elec-
tion. I was for Kennedy, but Glenn kept telling me that was stupid. It
happened that for some reason or other I had to vote absentee. The
polling place was a nearby bank, where a glamorous-looking (to my
eyes) secretary in a black dress checked my identification and gave me
a ballot. The whole process was unfamiliar, of course, and Doug was
wiggling and lurching about in my arms. She saw that I was having
quite a struggle, and offered to hold him. Immediately her black dress

was covered with white fuzz. Horrified, keenly aware of my own shabby appearance, I fled to the car. What was worse, at the last minute I had caved in and voted for Nixon! It shows who I was in those years.

THE HOUSTON PLAN

When our lease on the house in Bellaire was up we bought (#8) a newly built tract house in a booming area called Sharpstown. At 1,450 square feet, it seemed big enough for a growing family—I was pregnant again—and I liked its "Houston plan," as people referred to the common layout of a tiny dead-end living room off to one side and a larger family room at the back. It had a sliding glass door to the yard.

There's an essay by Alice Munro in which she talks about houses as a metaphor for writing. The part of the essay that particularly stays with me is this: "Everybody knows what a house does, how it encloses space and makes connections between one enclosed space and another and presents what is outside in a new way. This is the nearest I can come to explaining what a story does." Our view of the world is shaped by the windows of our houses, both the real ones we inhabit and the ones we build in our minds.

There in the Sharpstown house, it was mainly the sliding glass door that was my window onto a larger world. Literally, it gave me a view of a dinky concrete patio and bare dirt awaiting grass sod, but figuratively it shaped my viewpoint and with it, my sense of what mattered. I saw life through the windows of suburbia in those years. I was unable to see much of anything beyond.

We shape the houses we live in every time we remodel or hang pictures on the walls or repaint. But they also shape us. Moving from house to house, arranging our furniture to suit new spaces, we also reconstruct ourselves. Five years out of high school, where I had been the girl at the top of the class, I had redefined myself as a hopeless drudge, a sad sack with no ambition beyond getting better furni-

October 1963, Alan on his bouncy horse at the Sharpstown house.

ture and a few clothes. True, I had all along been taking correspondence courses—the distance education of the day—but my hope of
finishing college had all but evaporated. I rarely even read a book.

Baby Alan was born that fall, the fall of 1961. I remember the
killer headache from the epidural, but I remember even better how
happy I was to have this beautiful, healthy baby. All the more
shock, then, when it turned out that he wasn't, exactly. He too
needed surgery. This time, thankfully, the problem was one that
could be corrected—pyloric stenosis, a twist blocking the exit end
of the stomach. At four weeks he began projectile vomiting. Six
days later he was operated on, the tissue blocking his pyloris was
cut, and he came home fixed. At a year old he was fat and cute,
with blond curls, and our backyard, now fully fenced and grassy,
gave him a place to play.

Mostly, though, my memories of that house are of disasters: the
mucky glue that kept oozing up in ridges between the asphalt tiles of
the family room and kitchen floor (the builder finally had to take it

up and start over); the next-door neighbor's house flooding when they were out of town at Christmas, when their water pipes in the attic froze and burst during a rare cold spell. We were the first to see the water sluicing over their foundation, and when we looked through a window we saw that the ceiling had fallen in. But those disasters were nothing compared to ours. Doug went blind.

We never knew what caused it, whether it was the spiking fever when he developed an infection around the shunt or the sudden surge of pressure when the shunt had to be removed to let the infection clear up or the powerful antibiotic that turned out to have a history of causing blindness or the case of measles he came down with at the same time. Whichever it was, or all of them together, the visual function of his brain was destroyed. My view out the sliding glass door had never looked so bleak as it did then.

TRANSFERRED AGAIN

Alan was still a toddler when the corporation reached into our lives again and sent us to Chicago. We rented (#9) a three-bedroom in the suburb of Arlington Heights. A very different place, but still much the same in that our lives still revolved around hospitals. On November 22, 1963, the day JFK was assassinated, we made a panicky run through early morning traffic to a hospital in the Loop, with Doug in hard convulsions all the way. The neighbor who took Alan in on short notice told me the bad news about the president when I made a short run home that afternoon to pick up a few things so I could stay overnight at the hospital.

That Christmas Eve, after dark, I sat on the couch crying, facing the fact that Doug was never going to be cured, and the problems arising from his birth defect were going to extend out into the future for all of us, beyond any knowable horizon line.

We had resumed our habit of driving around and looking at houses, of course, and when our lease was up we bought another. It was a raw tract house (#10) in another new development. This one was a big shell of a house, bi-level, with a cavernous basement that Glenn planned to finish out. I tried to make the place attractive and homey, but with scarcely a penny to spare—we were always paying medical bills, or trying to—I didn't get very far. Fortunately, Mother sent me the old but still very good living room "draw drapes" she'd had made to match the pungent green walls in the remodeled rock house on Richardson Street. When they moved to their new house, she must have thought those drapes were just too expensive to throw away, and sure enough, now they came in handy. When closed, they shut out every gleam of light, but I didn't mind it at the time. I do remember how keenly disappointed I was with the tacky, improvised look of the green-and-yellow Con-Tact® paper I put up around the kitchen stove after the unwashable flat paint the builder had used got quickly spotted up. That sticky paper must have been quite something for the next owners to get rid of.

What else do I remember from that sad house? The wind that blew summer and winter. The snow that piled up in our down-sloping driveway. The displaced field mice that infested the house—I can still see the tip of a tail disappearing down the stairs. The way Alan, at only three, began to assume a caretaker role toward Doug. When offered a cookie, he said "not unless my brother can have one too." Glenn's blow-ups and frequent, unexplained absences. He went missing the whole rest of the day when baby Rick was born early one August morning, neglected even to phone my mother, who had come by train from Texas to take care of Doug and Alan, to tell her it was a boy and baby and mother were fine. It was years before I realized that he had seized the opportunity to spend an uninterrupted day with his girlfriend—not the longest-lasting of his affairs, but as he later told me himself, the most intense.

Rick was a fine, whole, healthy baby, needing no surgeries at all—a welcome change that I must have found energizing, because I got back to my studies. I remember sitting at the kitchen table of that wind-battered house on the bare plains, writing Latin lessons with my right hand while nursing him on the left. This was the last credit by correspondence that would count toward a degree, so I needed to figure out a way to get to an actual campus, but couldn't see a way to do it

At Thanksgiving, Glenn took some vacation time, and we made a car trip to Fort Worth. While we were there, Doug developed a new problem that none of our doctors could or would diagnose: rapid and shallow breathing. Dr. Blanche spoke to me about letting go. "Maybe it's time," she said. Instead, we left Alan with Mother and Dad and started the long drive back with Doug gasping in the back seat all the way. In southern Illinois we ran into an ice storm that had closed the roads, and had to spend an unplanned night in a motel, and I swiped a woolen crib blanket when we left the next morning because I was worried about keeping the baby warm. As soon as we got home, before the furnace had even warmed up the house, I phoned our neurosurgeon. "Lay the phone down," he said, "take a clock or watch with a second hand, and count his breaths for one minute." When I reported the number, he said to go straight to the hospital.

The shunt—a different kind now, draining into the chest cavity —was overstraining his heart. A pediatric heart specialist was called in, the shunt was removed, and the doctors sent him home to die with a neat triangle cut in the side of his head as a drain for the spinal fluid. For days he lay semi-comatose. Then on Christmas morning, as we were sitting hopelessly in the kitchen, we heard his voice and, running to his room, found him sitting up, demanding tomato juice.

His doctors had always said that if they could keep him alive long enough the natural circulation between skull and spine would open. Apparently it had. But the damage had been done. He was blind and mentally impaired and so unstable behaviorally or emotionally that the least thing could trigger screaming rages during which he beat the sides of his head with his fists or clawed his cheeks until the blood ran. These days he would probably be called autistic.

Life was hard there, hard as the icy winters. Depression settled in so thickly that I scarcely noticed when Glenn told me things were unsettled at the office. My mind was fixed on one day at a time. That fall we had planted a little crabapple tree in front of the house, but we never got to see it bloom because before spring came, a corporate buy-out shook up our lives once again. Glenn could have accepted a transfer to Los Angeles, but he didn't think it looked promising. Instead, he looked for another job and quickly found one with Gulf Oil. Off we went to Port Arthur, Texas.

I didn't like the sound of the place and didn't want to go, but he dangled a powerfully attractive bait in front of me: There was a college in nearby Beaumont. We would live there, he would commute, and I could go back to college.

THE PINE TREE HOUSE

In the spring of 1965, we bought (#11) an attractive three-bedroom colonial, not as big as the house in Illinois, but more livable, and in a pleasant, settled neighborhood. It had a wonderful back-yard with dense grass and azalea bushes and great tall pine trees, and a little boy next door for Alan to play with. And that summer I started back to school, taking a full-time load to try to move this along. Rick was seven months old; it wasn't easy. When I made a D that fall on the first exam in second-semester German (there had been an eight-year gap since first-semester German), I carried it on top of my notebook as a reminder of what could happen.

That same fall, Doug started first grade. I have a snapshot of him in his raincoat, boarding the school bus with the driver holding his hand. How his truly heroic teacher managed I do not know. The screaming fits that had started in his second year were unrelenting.

Rick in the piney backyard of the Beaumont house on a good day.

Now he had taken to throwing things at people (once he threw a chair at me), and he had a puzzling way of getting started at something, some repetitive action, and going on and on as if he literally could not stop himself. This was something he had done all his life. We knew it wasn't right, but when I asked a pediatrician about it once, he had looked at me as if I were crazy. But now, when I summoned up my nerve and asked the school-district psychologist, he not only didn't cast a funny look at me, he had a name for it: perseverating. Very common in children with brain damage, he said. Very predictable that Doug would do that as well as overreact to noises and have screaming fits. It was comforting to know that I hadn't been crazy. It wasn't that I had not known how to nurture him.

Glenn's way of dealing with the turmoil at home caused by Doug's problems had always been to stay away for hours after work or on Saturdays. His blow-ups, yelling, and name-calling continued as before, only now, he was coming in with slurred speech more often, and he was overspending. We went ever deeper and deeper in debt. If he made five dollars, he spent eight; if he got a raise to eight, he spent fourteen. I never understood it.

My secret plan in returning to college had been to get a teaching job as soon as I finished and get a divorce. Probably I wouldn't have had the nerve to carry it out; confrontations were not my strong suit. But anyway, that was my plan. But when the English department offered me a teaching fellowship, whatever that was, if I would stay on for an M.A., I couldn't resist. I stayed in school, picked up a little extra money by substitute teaching, and stayed in the marriage.

And then Steven came along, another precious baby and another reason to stay.

#12

Again we were transferred to Houston, and again we bought a brand new house on a bare dirt lot. Alan and Rick didn't want to move, of course, so this time Glenn dangled some bait in front of them. He promised them a go-cart or dirt bike to ride in the undeveloped area that would be across the side street from us. The promise lapsed almost as soon as it was spoken; maybe they had known it would; but they did enjoy rambling in the woods.

Alan proved to be just as loving to the new baby as he had been to Doug. I have a snapshot of him sitting in a rocking chair in the new family room, giving baby Steven his bottle, and another that shows him standing tall and straight in the bare backyard in his Cub Scout uniform. But why does he look so sad-eyed? For all of his compassion and hold-it-together attitude, those eyes tell the tale of what was really going on in our household.

By this time I had finished my M.A., but having once gotten a taste of graduate school I couldn't stop. I loved reading, attending small classes, writing papers, and discussing critical approaches. I started on my Ph.D. that fall.

Glenn was not pleased; he wanted me to get a real job and make some money. It's ironic, I suppose, that I complain about all the transfers and the moving when it was those very moves that let me continue in this path and thus reinvent myself as a person with my own goals and achievements—though I still harbored the same fear of confrontation and conflict.

There was plenty that needed confronting. With this move Glenn had launched into an affair that would go on for years. So now, along with everything else, there was this woman in the middle of our marriage. He presented her as a friend from work and brought her into our home for dinners and family occasions. And the thing was, she pretended to be my friend too. And I went along with the pretense, denying even to myself the truth of what I instinctively knew. Sometimes I resolved to call them on it, but mostly I just stewed.

Retreating and trying to ignore what was happening—all that was happening—was so much easier than launching into the major argument that I knew would come. The few times I did accuse Glenn, he told me I was crazy and needed a psychiatrist. Sometimes I wondered if it was true. It all got more and more tangled. He even brought her in one Christmas morning. As soon as we opened presents he rushed off "to pick something up at the store," stayed away for more than an hour, and returned with her in tow. She sat on one of the barstools and complained that Steven's new pull-toy was too noisy. Yet even then I didn't say what needed to be said. Four children, one of them severely handicapped, what could I do but deny?

The Tree-House House

In the middle of the fall semester of 1971, when I was finishing my course requirements, we were whisked away by another transfer, this time to the Gulf refinery in Philadelphia. We made a hasty house looking trip, and then Glenn went on to start the job while I stayed behind until the end of January to wind things up. I moved my comprehensive exams up by four months, got a dissertation proposal in, and packed boxes to move.

When the children and I went up, we stayed the first few weeks in a short-term suite-hotel (#13), until we could take possession of the house. I didn't know until later that Glenn had had the "Other Woman" up for a visit in the same suite.

House #14 was not another tract house but a well-established and comfortable split-level on a rolling half-acre in Delaware County. I would guess it's the place my sons think of when they hear the word "home"—if they think of anywhere.

It was a wonderful place to live, really, with its green expanses and its birch tree in front, and its forsythia and tulips in the spring and friendly neighbors all around. Best of all, there was a tree house in back where the boys could play and have sleep-outs. In bad weather they played games or watched TV in the cozy family room while I worked on my dissertation, but mostly they were out ranging over the neighborhood with friends. They quickly learned to ice skate, and they delighted in sledding on the bigger slopes in neighbors' yards, especially a certain forbidden hill where the owner would emerge from his house yelling at them to go away. In summer they freely roamed a large wooded park that began behind the houses on the other side of the street, and at least once, though I didn't know it until later, caught the trolley into Philadelphia for a brief ramble around the 69th Street Station. Our neighborhood seemed so safe, and they always seemed like such good, responsible kids that I didn't worry when they stayed out a long time, I just thought they were having fun in the park.

Their schools were good, too. Rick started trombone lessons, the beginning of his life's work. Alan shot up in height and accumulated reprimands for jumping to touch the ceilings (as well as, less benignly, for failing to do homework). Steven was already exhibiting the brightness that would be a challenge to nurture adequately. And Doug was at the fine Overbrook School for the Blind during the week, coming home on weekends. Summers, he spent two weeks at a vacation home for blind children at the Jersey Shore. So in some ways it was a good time for him too. We took him to Phillies games and to the Eagles training camp, to shake hands with the players. But

The house in Pennsylvania.

Steven and our dog Pokey with the tree house in the background.

it was also a bad time for him. He began to understand things. The worst moment of all was the time he screamed out in one of his rages, "I'm tired of being blind!" What do you say to that? There was nothing; there is nothing.

So this house too was haunted: by Doug's disability and behavior problems that sent Steven hiding under the bed; by Glenn's drinking and his temper outbursts, his constant overspending and the unrelenting load of debt; by the corrosive presence of the woman in the guise of family friend. She had managed to wangle a transfer to Pittsburgh, allowing her to come visit fairly easily, and I was beginning not only to resent these visits but also to resist them. I told him I didn't want her to stay with the kids the weekend I was to go along with him on a semi-business, semi-pleasure kind of trip. He arranged for her to come anyway. I told him I didn't want her invited for various holidays; he invited her anyway.

Even with all this, there were some good times. We played croquet, we set up a badminton net and had family tournaments, we went to the neighborhood Fourth of July party. All in all, it was probably our best time as a family, even with all the negatives. And it was largely the house and its setting, conducive to outside pleasures and wide neighborhood interaction, that made it so.

I finished my degree and taught for two years at Bryn Mawr and a year at Haverford College—temporary part-time appointments with no future in them, but at a time of scarcity in the academic job market, let alone at such good places, anyone who had a job at all felt lucky. I was scheduled to be at Haverford for a second year in the fall of 1975 when, of course, Glenn was transferred again, back to Port Arthur. Strange as it seems, it never even occurred to me to say "I'm not going; I'm staying here with the boys and keeping my job." Wives were just supposed to go along. Anyway, I couldn't have supported us on my part-time teaching. I would have had to search for a real job and be prepared to move anywhere I could find one, and at a time when (so it was reported) there were four hundred applicants for every opening in an English department, I didn't even try.

BACK TO TEXAS

Instead of living in Beaumont again, we chose Port Neches, a smaller town that would mean a shorter commute. It also meant liv-

ing with the smell of chemical plants in the air, instead of the flowering trees we'd been enjoying, and schools nowhere near as good as
ones the boys were coming from. On Rick's first day he asked the
other children whether they went on field trips. He was remembering his school outings to the Liberty Bell, to Valley Forge. "Where
would we go?" they asked. Good question.

We moved into an apartment (#15) while we had a house built.
All I remember of that apartment is the shouting matches of the cou-
ple downstairs and the multitude of roaches in the kitchen. And that
Glenn wanted to invite Marie (as I'll call her) over from Houston
(she'd also been transferred back) for Christmas. For once, I put my
foot down. "This apartment is too small to bring her in," I said.
"She'll get in the way." In more ways than one, I could have added.
He was mad. He told me what a bad person I was and how lonely she
was going to be, all alone at Christmas, but for once he backed down.
He didn't invite her.

January and February were rainy, and it seemed to take forever
to get the house finished. Finally we moved into (#16) a roomy two-
story on a corner lot. Visually, my memories of it are sketchy: a
mansard roof, a brick fireplace, "velvet" wallpaper in the entry. It
doesn't matter.

Doug had been fine with this move; it meant he could go back to
the school he remembered so well in Austin. But Alan and Rick
hadn't liked the idea any better than I had. They'd had the best friends
of their lives in Pennsylvania. So once again Glenn had dangled some
bait: we would get an Irish Setter puppy. This time he kept his promise. We bought a beautiful puppy, named her Cinnamon, and quickly
found out that she was the wildest ball of energy on four legs that any
of us had ever seen. We had no idea how to control her. Steven simply
refused to go in the backyard if she was off her chain. We sold her to a
teenage boy who thought her wildness was wonderful.

Life in Port Neches was a bad time for us all. The best thing
about Alan's high school was its winning football team. Sports were

the be-all and end-all, and Alan wasn't a jock. He did play in the marching band, but when he tried to sign up for intramural basketball the coach made it clear that outsiders weren't welcome. It was really a conditioning program for the football players. Rick, now in junior high and hanging around with a bad crowd, tried to construct himself as a tough guy by cultivating a perpetual snarl. Only his trombone saved him. However far off target he got otherwise, he still practiced, he was still centered. Steven's elementary school didn't even have a library. When we asked, the principal said just have him say what book he wanted and they would order it. The idea of having a second grader plan the school library struck me as a trifle odd. As for me, I once again picked up some part-time teaching, this time at a weak branch campus of Lamar in a nearby town. Quite a change.

No, I didn't build up any affection for that place. Or for the neighbors who stood in a circle to watch and prevent interference when their boys got into fights after school. And certainly they didn't build up any affection for me.

But the corporate revolving door went round again, and we got out of there and back to Houston and yet another new house (#17) on the far west edge of the city. All in all, this was our nicest house yet. That was the idea, of course, that the houses should get steadily better as the salary went up. Another positive aspect of the move was that I was asked to teach a part-time schedule at Rice, back where I'd done my Ph.D. work. It was clear I could never be anything but an adjunct there—they didn't hire their own for tenure-track positions—but at least I was back at a good place. The main negative was that once again the boys had to break off friendships and start over in different schools—probably a good thing this time, but nevertheless unsettling for them.

Once again we were faced with putting in a new lawn on a bare dirt lot, but surprisingly, Glenn didn't seem to mind. I found out later that Marie actually came and helped him put in sod while the kids and I were back in Port Neches getting ready to move. Incredible.

THE HOUSE ON BRAXTONSHIRE

After only a year in that nice new house that was stretching our budget to the breaking point, we moved to a more prestigious area in the wooded northwest and to an even nicer new house (#18) that stretched it even more. The only reason to move this time was that some other people in the company, whom we'd known several years, had been transferred to Houston shortly after we were and had bought in a beautiful subdivision out that way, and Glenn couldn't stand to be eclipsed. He fretted and stomped around and found fault with things he'd previously thought were outstanding features. So once again, and quite needlessly, the boys were pulled out of schools they liked and dropped down in unfamiliar ones. My parents, who had worked hard to keep their mouths shut over the years, said, "This is ridiculous!" I agreed, but went along, entering right into the spirit of things and choosing even better wallpapers

Alan, reading in the family room of the house on Braxtonshire.

than I had the time before. We sold our maple dining room furniture and bought a new set with chair seats upholstered in gold velvet. It was a gold velvet kind of house.

The neighborhood was a kind of Camelot, insulated from the social realities of the larger world. But even Camelot had varmints. There were possums that snarled from the corner of the garage, armadillos that uprooted the shrubs and left them to die, and poisonous snakes—rattlers, copperheads—that had a habit of imperiling small animals and children. But looking back on it, I find it fitting for those varmints to be living in such a posh neighborhood. It seemed that the more Glenn got into the upper layers of the marketing arm of the company, the more varmints showed up at corporate social functions too. I had never been very good at the role of executive's wife, and as I saw less and less to like in that role, I cared less and less about trying. More than once he complained that he was ashamed of me at company functions because I didn't wear the right clothes or the right makeup or talk about the right things.

My teaching at Rice had morphed by then into full-time administrative work. I was belatedly starting to have a career of my own. The downside was, it meant a long daily commute and coming in tired just in time to start dinner. I wasn't home when the boys came in from school and wasn't as involved in their lives as I should have been. It bothered me then and bothers me now. Those years pass so quickly, and you can't go back and do them over. Oh, I was happy for what they were doing and gave them abundant praise, but I didn't go see their bands march at halftime (two different high schools, two bands), even when Rick played solos, and the only time I can remember doing anything at Steven's school was once when I took our Braille writer to his enrichment class so he could demonstrate it—the Braille writer on which I wrote letters to Doug, still in school at Austin.

Certainly their father didn't do those things. So the boys pretty much ran their own lives. Alan took a job delivering pizza, then worked at a grocery store where he sat in the parking lot after clos-

ing time and drank beer. Rick became (to Glenn's great embarrass-
ment) a cook in a neighborhood cafe. He lined up trombone lessons
with a member of the symphony and arranged for one of his friends
at school to give Steven trumpet lessons. Of course, they still turned
to me for some things. When Rick managed to scrape a fender on the
iron fence beside the driveway, I arranged to get both car and fence
fixed quickly while Glenn was out of town, to protect him from the
storm we both knew would land on him for it. It was our secret.

I was overwhelmed, unhappy, and detached. I hid behind books
to avoid interacting. To block out the parts of my life that were out
of control, I sat on the bedroom floor with the door closed and wrote.
Writing and reading were my refuge. They were also, I suppose, my
passive aggression. I was nerving myself to end the marriage. But
even with all that had gone before, it took a couple of precipitating
incidents to send me out the door.

The first of these was truly ugly. It happened at the dinner table
when, with no warning and in front of company, Glenn slapped
eleven-year-old Steven across the face. Rick's best friend, Jerry, was
spending a week with us, and I had cooked that classic Texas menu,
chicken-fried steak and gravy. I am never a reliable gravy maker.
Either it comes out too thick or too thin, or there's too much or too
little. That night it tasted good but there wasn't enough. And something Glenn could never bear was scantiness at the table, I suppose
for fear someone would think we didn't always have an abundance.
It must have been an insecurity that sprang from some deep hurt, but
if so, that hurt was inaccessible to me. I only knew the results, the
times when he got up from the table and stalked away in a fury. This
time he had taken the gravy bowl out of Steven's hands and spooned
a little onto his plate himself, just a dab, to hide the fact that there
wasn't a lot in the bowl. Steven asked for more, and he hit him.
When I saw Steven rush from the table in tears and saw the shocked
looks on the other boys' faces, I knew I had to get them out of there.
Yet still, for a while longer, I hung in there.

Only now as I write this do I see the parallel: I had seen my mother lift her hand to slap a five-year-old for asking when she would bring his piece of chicken. Now Glenn had slapped an eleven-year-old the same way and for the same trifling cause, asking for food at the table. They were both, I believe, impelled by deep rage and insecurity. And I needed to get out of the house of my marriage as urgently as I had needed to escape the house of my childhood.

The second precipitating incident was minor by comparison. But sometimes it's a little thing that provides a spark. Hanging up laundry one day, I found a suede sports coat in Glenn's closet, still in the store bag. He had slipped it in without mentioning it. As I looked at that expensive jacket, it represented for me the great gap between us in how we thought of possessions and value. I stood there and thought how hard I struggled every month to pay the bills, even now, when his salary had soared and I was bringing in my bit as well. And at that, I was only paying the minimum on the credit cards. I counted the suits and sports coats in his closet, the multiple pairs of expensive shoes. And I knew that was the end.

When I confronted him that night, he said yeah, well, spending what he had for the suede jacket hadn't hurt the family any because he'd paid for it by taking a little here and a little there on expense accounts—as if that made it OK, as if it was going to make me think better of him.

After that moment I never looked back. As for house #18, as nice as it was, probably the nicest house I would ever live in, I knew I wasn't going to miss it a bit. I'd never felt at home there in the least. How could I, when I didn't feel at home in my life? But now I was ready to change all that.

CHAPTER THREE

Something Completely Different

S O IT WAS THAT at the age of forty-two I prepared to become single for, in a very real sense, the first time in my life, and prepared to move into my very own place for the first time.

The boys reacted to the news in very different and somewhat puzzling ways. Alan apparently hadn't seen this coming at all. Home for the summer after his first year of college, he went in and out to his two part-time jobs with a deer-caught-in-the-headlights look. Doug, for all his limitations, had been more perceptive and was less surprised. "I knew it!" he burst out. "I knew this was going to happen if he didn't stop that yelling at you!" It was hard not to feel a little smug. Rick more or less took it in stride, with no questions, no outbursts, and, as far as I could tell, no great upset. Caught up in a swirl of senior year and job and steady girlfriend, he went about his business with his usual independence, getting himself to the doctor when he had some health issues and quietly sending off his application to Rice as a music major. Steven was the one who most worried me. As the youngest, it was his life that was being the most thoroughly disrupted. He reacted by bottling it up inside and going around tense and quiet—so much like his mother.

Now it was going to be up to me to make the money to pay bills, keep the yard mowed, and set the tone. I was not only going to have to lower our standard of living, I wanted to. But with Rick going into his senior year of high school and Steven his next-to-last year of middle school, I didn't want them to have to change schools. So I took a lease on a two-story house on Westminster Circle in the same subdivision as the house on Braxtonshire. It was bigger than we needed and more expensive than I could afford, so not a good start on my plans for a new life according to a different set of values, but I didn't want them to have to change schools.

The house had a living room, spacious dining room, and an eat-in kitchen down, and three bedrooms up. I offered Alan and Rick the largest of these, the "master," with its own bath, and Steven and I took the two smaller ones and shared the hall bath. My room also had a little adjoining sitting area where I could sew or grade papers in quiet when I wanted to, how I wanted to. The gold velvet dining room set was staying with its master, so we decided to use the dining room as a music room—a good trade-off.

We did the moving ourselves. No way was I going to spend a chunk of my modest nest-egg hiring movers! Alan drove the U-Haul, discovering only when we pulled out onto a busy road that he didn't know how to shift the gears. He managed somehow, and we got it back to the house and started loading up. Rick's friend Jerry was visiting again, and worked as hard as anyone. Still, I had been afraid the boys wouldn't be able to manage the piano and had reluctantly accepted Glenn's offer to help with it, but that was all, nothing else. Bringing in the piano was the only time he ever passed through that door. Once it was safely off the van and inside, he lingered on the porch to ask if he could he stay with us for a couple of weeks while he got settled elsewhere, but I said no, quickly and clearly. This was my house, mine and the boys', not his.

The next day when I went back to check around for anything we might have missed, I let myself in through the back and had started looking around the kitchen when I realized I was hearing something from the other part of the house. It was Marie, there cleaning up while Glenn got in a round of golf. A pair of his old house shoes flopped on her feet, and her hair was down in her face. We looked at each other a long minute. She didn't bother flashing a smile this time. "The vacuum cleaner isn't working right," she said at last.

Outside my first house as a single adult. How young I was!

"Too bad," I told her, and left. She was on her own.

The music room we'd set up in our new dining room was a great success. It provided a nice big space for Rick to practice trombone or Steven to practice trumpet. After resisting piano lessons for years, he was now taking it up on his own, teaching himself to play much as he had earlier taught himself to type. Right after we moved he pulled out some old piano method books left from when I used to give lessons and started systematically working his way through them. While I made dinner after work in the evening, I might dash in from the kitchen to offer a suggestion or two, but essentially he did it on his own. I suppose it was a coping mechanism. He might be having some anxiety about the divorce, but he could teach himself to play the piano.

Whether the boys ever felt really at home there I don't know, but I thought we were quite cozy. We lived without conflict—no more walking on eggshells, no yelling, no name-calling. It was amazing how peaceful day-to-day life could be. For weeks I went around singing a phrase from a current song, either in my head or right out loud: "I never thought I could feel so free."

The one bad part, besides the rent, was that I still had the same long commute. I looked forward to moving closer in when the boys' school situation was resolved. At least I was liking my job at the university, though. My boss pretty much let me do what I thought was important and skip the busywork that I thought wasn't. As director of graduate programs I got acquainted with faculty members all around the campus, especially those in charge of the graduate programs in their departments. They were all interesting, and most were also nice to work with.

One of the nicest was the professor in charge of graduate studies in civil engineering. We interacted frequently on acceptances or rejections of applications, awards of fellowships or assistantships, problem-solving, acceptance of dissertations—the usual processes of graduate education. One day when I called him about some matter and started my usual "Dr. Lutes, this is—" he surprised me by interrupting with "Yes, Janis."

I didn't quite know what to think of this man. Tall, bearded, shaggy-haired, he seemed composed of equal parts friendliness and shyness. When he came to my office, he stood against the wall with his hands behind his back, as if to say "Look, no hands, don't mind me, I can't do a thing." I remarked about it to my secretary one day, "Dr. Lutes is sort of odd, don't you think?"

She tilted her head to one side, considering it. "But very nice," she said.

And I realized more and more that it was true. I began to understand his hands-behind-back gesture as indicating not so much insecurity as a non-aggressive nature, a gentleness.

Not long after the boys and I moved, then, and while the divorce was in progress, Loren and I went to lunch together. Mainly I told him my troubles. I knew he had been divorced for a year or so and would probably have some wisdom to share. And he did. Then after a few weeks we went to a play together. Then a picnic during lunch hour. He brought pictures of his children—two teenage boys, two little girls. He watched closely as he handed me the picture of the youngest, Rebekah. She was black, or more accurately, mixed-race. Was he telling me he'd had an affair with some young black woman and gotten her pregnant and then not stayed with her? I would find that very troubling indeed! I didn't know what to say. "She's adopted," he said. "We wanted Laura to have a little sister." So I'd been on the wrong track completely! "She's a real cutie," I said. "If I'd ever had a girl, I would have named her Rebecca."

I had passed the test. If I had reacted negatively to her race, there wouldn't have been any point going further.

After that we had an evening picnic at a concert in the park, where we got Steven together with the girls. And by then I knew that as much as I liked being single for the first time in my life, there was something else I would like even better. Ten months after my divorce we were married, with my parents and brother and all eight kids in attendance. We were embarking on a completely different way of living, for both of us—or I should say, for all ten of us.

The First Year

We would have liked to look for a place close to campus, but we didn't want to disrupt Steven's school situation. He would be changing to start high school in another year anyway. This meant that after living five minutes from his office, Loren voluntarily undertook a long commute through fierce traffic. One of my longtime friends told me, "I can't believe he would take on all that driving just to marry you." I chose to believe she meant it in fun. Not only did he drive back and forth to work five days a week, but there were extra round trips every other weekend when the girls came and even more if they had weekend school activities or parties. He never told them no. Because he loved me, because he loved them, because he wanted to fulfill his parental role, he drove back and forth, back and forth. It wasn't easy for him. But after all, a year isn't a very long time.

We could have stayed on in the house I'd already been leasing. The owners were going to be out of the country for another year anyway, and that would have been by far the easier thing to do. But we felt that if we stayed there, it would go on seeming like my place, and Loren would be put in the position of guest or even perhaps, in Steven's eyes, intruder. It didn't seem like the right way to start the marriage.

Then too, we were worried about money. Each of us, separately, had been barely scraping by as it was, and now we would have the "marriage tax." So we took a year's lease on a house in a less expensive but still nearby neighborhood zoned to the same middle school—next door, in fact, to one of Steven's friends. It was considerably smaller and simpler than the house where I'd spent my one year single. I remember especially how crowded the eating area was. When the girls came for weekends, we had to squeeze in. But we were glad we'd done it.

I was telling my editor all this one day over lunch (the editor of the press that was publishing my first novel) and she observed that I seemed to be engaged in downward mobility. It was true, and it was intentional—un-American as that may seem. Downward mobility felt like liberation

The House on Darnell

At the end of the school year, with Steven ready for high school, we bought our first house together, a half-hour's drive from campus. It was an unassuming single-story three-bedroom, not particularly striking in any way. I felt at home from the day we moved in.

Becoming a family: Laura, Steven, Rebekah, me, and Loren.
The cat's name was Orpheus.

We liked that house a lot. We liked its location, its layout, its yard, and the distinguished old gentleman next door who liked to stand and talk. We liked the space behind the garage where I made a garden. Once Loren trimmed it, we liked the hedge beside the walk from the driveway to the front door.

I want to linger a moment over that house that was so important in shaping our new life, room by room. It had a comfortable living room, neither small nor very large, which we improved by adding bookshelves on both sides of the wide casement door to the family room, on the back. It wasn't a very attractive family room, with its stale vinyl floor, but a big glass door offered a view of a covered patio and nice greenery, and once we added some tweedy carpet and a plaid sofa bought with my parents' house-warming gift it became quite inviting. Off to the right, the family room opened onto a sunny eating area with bright floral wallpaper, which led to the U-shaped kitchen overlooking the front walk. There too a little improvement was needed. The cabinets were drab and thirsty-looking. So in our second year in the house I scrubbed them with de-glazer and painted them pale yellow inside and out. How I got up the nerve to tackle such a project I don't know; I'd never done such a thing in my life. It took three coats. But what a transformation!

The bedrooms, all rather unremarkable, were strung front to back along the east side of the house. Steven's, on the front, the north, was drafty, so we bought him a little portable heater. The middle one was for Laura and Beka's weekends; we brightened it up with new bedspreads. Our room, on the back with its own tiny bath, was fine, not too big and not too small, not fancy but not shabby, just right.

We settled into the business of being a family. Doug was living in a group home in San Angelo and working at the Lighthouse for the Blind there. Steven had been admitted to the High School for the Performing Arts and rode a bus that picked him up and dropped him off at Bellaire High, only a couple of blocks from us. Laura was one year ahead of him at the same school, also in music (French horn). Rick and Alan were both at Rice, for that year at least, though Rick would soon go off to the Curtis Institute of Music in Philadelphia. Dan, Loren's oldest, was also at Rice, about to graduate and go into the navy. David, his next oldest, hadn't gone to college after high school, but seemed to be finding his way. Beka, the youngest, was having some problems in school but so far nothing that seemed serious. All eight (eight kids! I couldn't get over it!) seemed to be on track. And it was so much easier for us to have the girls with us on weekends now that Loren didn't have to drive clear across the city to pick them up and take them back.

One weekend soon after we moved in something happened that, for the five of us who were there at the time, entered our family lore. On Saturday night about midnight Laura and Beka came to our bedroom door and reported that they had heard screaming from the house next door. It sounded like someone was being murdered! Then we heard it too, a screaming punctuated by crashes. Something came hurtling through a side window onto the neighbor's driveway adjacent to our bedrooms. About that time Steven came to join us, and we debated whether Loren should go to the door to see what was wrong. It seemed like a bad idea. He called the police.

We stood in a tight knot on the sidewalk while two policemen walked around the house looking in windows, trying to figure out what was going on. There was a woman in there, they said, who appeared to be running from room to room throwing and breaking things. Broken glass was all over the floor, and she was running around barefoot, getting blood all over the place. Did we know where her husband might be? No, no idea. They called an ambulance and went in and took her away. And we never knew any more about it.

If the windows of houses can frame the world we look out on, as Alice Munro says they do, they can also frame the view in for those standing outside. The window over the driveway that our neighbor had broken out when she was throwing things framed a view into a life of bizarre and disturbing misery. We were thankful that life inside our own house was nothing like that at all.

We enjoyed that first house we owned together. We grew more green beans, okra, and tomatoes in that little plot behind the garage than I could believe, okra so tall I had to bend the stalks down to reach the pods. There was also a fig tree in back that put on a spectacle of abundance every year (though none of us cared for figs). Even our cats liked living there. They stalked birds and enjoyed chasing the wooden croquet balls when we set up the wickets for weekend games. I don't mean life was problem-free; there were frustrations at work, and we had our worries. But we got along, that was the important thing. Steven's piano studies blossomed at a startling rate under the guidance of a fine teacher. Laura found a steady boyfriend we liked a lot (still do, as a son-in-law) and gave a senior recital that made us proud. She and Beka still came for weekends. Our finances, which we had expected to be tight, were surprisingly healthy. We bought a certificate of deposit, and then another.

54

Loren playing banjo at our first home, on Darnell.

This is something we've never quite understood. We went into our marriage expecting it to be a close call financially, but from the very first month our income always exceeded our expenses. Our salaries were modest, and it wasn't that we were scrimping, but at the end of a month the balance in the checkbook would be up from the month before. This, too, was a welcome change—not to be piling up debt, not to be living with a goal of buying, buying, buying; getting more, more, more; moving up; impressing people. And not only was our financial stability important for our peace of mind at the time, but as it turned out, it helped long-term. When the time came to retire, we had been free of a house payment for five years and the money we had saved could go into our retirement home.

We were doing well, then, and we liked where we were living, but nevertheless, a few years into our marriage, we found ourselves dissatisfied at work. Loren was now department chair but felt—and was—under-appreciated and under-rewarded. He had stayed too long at the same university, I suppose, and it was easy for them to take him for granted. As for my job in the graduate office, it was low-paying, and we knew it would never lead to a real faculty appointment. The fact that I was publishing books and articles at a fast clip was never going to matter; I was never going to escape my adjunct status. I was their own student and had come in on a staff job. So we started responding to job ads, hoping somehow to work out a dual move.

The change, when it came, didn't come about as a result of our inquiries, though, but by invitation. A letter arrived inviting me to apply for an associate dean job at Texas A&M that would also carry tenure as an associate professor—a truly miraculous change of status, considering that I'd never held a "real" faculty position. I went for an interview, they made me the offer, we agreed on terms, and Loren was also made an offer. Even more miraculous, in my opinion, was his willingness to change jobs for the sake of advancing my career. We accepted, and after five years in our pleasant little house on Darnell, put it on the market.

LIGHT AND BRIGHT AND OPEN

The university offered to put us in touch with a real estate agent to help us find a place to live, and when she phoned she asked what were the main qualities I wanted in a house. I didn't have to stop and think: it had to be light and bright and open. Almost without my realizing it, those had become my requirements. And they still are. I can understand the charms of enclosure—a dimly lit den with bookshelves all around, dark paneling agleam from lamps placed within easy reach, and cozy recesses. I can understand it, but it's not for me. What I want is lots of windows and white ceilings. Maybe this has its roots in that too-green living room in the remodeled house of my childhood.

So we made a weekend trip to College Station (and its neighboring town, Bryan), and knew as soon as we walked into the fourth place the realtor showed us, on Twisted Oaks Circle, that this was our house. Its placement high above the cul-de-sac street—high in comparison to the usual flatness of Bryan—with its driveway curving sharply uphill between low brick walls gave it a striking appearance. The door opened onto an open entry hall and a living room whose sloped ceiling soared up to a two-story window on the back wall. Straight in front of the door, an open staircase went up from the entry to a small sitting room with a balcony rail on the second floor. A shuttered bar and a storage space were tucked under the stairs, and beyond it a light and bright dining room with its own tall windows. The master bedroom, on the front of the house, had a big window overlooking the slope down to the street. I would spend hours at the corner desk in front of that window, looking out into treetops. In late fall, cedar waxwings flew in and out of the bushes under the window.

The homey house in Bryan.

We would have made an offer on the spot if we hadn't thought that would be imprudent. So we waited a week, came back to see it again, and bought it.

This time we didn't have to do our own moving, so it was easy, on us at any rate. Our cats didn't seem to agree. When the movers came, one of them managed to claw his way out of the cardboard carrier we had bought at the veterinarian's and hide behind the refrigerator. He jumped out as it was lifted onto a dolly and nearly caused the mover to fall over, refrigerator and all. We stuffed this cat into the fiberglass carrier where the other one had been, and thinking he was calmer, put him into the cardboard box. Before we got two miles down the road, he had also clawed his way out and they both yowled in outrage from the back seat. During the night, after we shut them in the hall bathroom while we went to a motel, they apparently tried to climb out at the ceiling—we found the lighting fixture over the sink knocked sideways the next morning. At least they hadn't clawed the wallpaper off the walls.

We moved in to the new house on a January day with fine snow in the air, a rare event and, we thought, a good omen.

Once again, we were very happy with the house we had chosen. We felt comfortably at home there from the first day. It had a lusciously green backyard with a good tree where Loren hung a bird-feeder that was visible from the kitchen. We had cardinals year-round, various sorts of sparrows, blue jays (too big for the perch, but they ate what fell to the ground), mockingbirds, black-tufted titmice, Carolina chickadees. There were also lots of squirrels as determined to get at the feeder as Loren was to keep them away.

Steven was in college now, so he was home only for holidays and one summer. When he was there, he had the entire upstairs to himself—bedroom, bath, and balconied sitting room. Unlike the rest of the house, the upstairs was very dark, with all its walls done in a wood paneling so dark it was nearly black. He called it The Cave.

Top: *One of many.*
Above: *Rebekah and her first, Joshua.*

THE FIRST GREEN BEDROOM

Loren and I don't think of ourselves as restless people. Yet after a few years at Texas A&M, for reasons that don't matter now, we again became dissatisfied in our jobs and tried—not so successfully this time—to make another dual-career move. Auburn University, in Alabama, was advertising for both a department head in civil engineering and a dean of liberal arts. We applied and were both invited for interviews. And Loren was offered the job. But I wasn't. They chose the inside candidate instead. After a flurry of phone calls from the newly selected dean, though, I agreed to go as associate dean. I didn't want to be an associate dean again, especially when it developed that, for reasons of strict legality, it had to be on an interim basis, pending a search. But Loren had been willing to move for my sake, so it seemed only fair that I should move for his. It didn't work out. When I was offered the permanent associate dean position, it didn't carry faculty status. And after so many years in marginalized positions, I wasn't willing to give that up.

But my point here is the house and what it taught us.

Since we went to Auburn fully expecting to stay, we went ahead and bought a house even though our house in Bryan hadn't yet sold. It was a beautiful house, showier than we were looking for as well as more expensive, but we liked it so much we indulged ourselves. Besides, there weren't many choices.

Our house in Auburn was striking from the curb and dramatic inside, the work of people who truly had an eye for design. We would never have been so bold with colors and combinations ourselves. There were good hardwood floors in the living room, dining room, and kitchen, dark green damask wallpaper in the dining room, white lacquer kitchen cabinets, and a bright breakfast room with pale yellow floral wallpaper and a bay window reaching almost to the floor. Light and bright indeed! And then the master bedroom, with walls painted a deep bluish-grayish-green that we would never have thought of selecting but immediately loved. A white bathroom with a huge over-the-tub window offering a view of grass and flowering bushes and a dogwood tree; there is probably nothing that gives me such a sense of well-being as dogwood in bloom.

I will never forget the yard we had there. Things grew in that soil! Besides, it had slopes and interest and had been beautifully planted with a seasonal succession of blooming things, including thirteen camellia bushes. Actually, there were only twelve when we moved in, because one had died, but we quickly replaced it with a Pink Perfection, my favorite. On a neglected slope at the end of the driveway we put in bearded iris that actually came up and bloomed. And there was a fine big deck where we could have sat and looked at it all—if only the weather hadn't been so hot and humid most of the time.

Living in that house in Auburn loosened up our decorative ideas. It was the first really well decorated house either of us had lived in. It led us to be a little more daring and taught us that we could not only create, but also indulge in, decorative pleasures. Though we lived there only a year, it had a real impact on the plans we began to draw up, several years later, for our retirement.

When my job didn't work out and we left (Loren never hesitated, even though his had worked out, and quite well) we returned to our house in Bryan with its high ceilings and its good back-yard tree for the bird feeder. We got painters in before the moving van arrived and had the cabinets as well as the upstairs paneling done over in white, like the ones in Auburn, and our bedroom painted the same green. We pulled down all the curtains and put up translucent shades, to let in even more light. We changed the wallpapers. And the small bedroom adjoining the kitchen became, in effect, my study, because Loren bought a second computer for upstairs, so we would no longer have to do a polite dance after dinner to see who got to use it. A lot of changes, really. But this house, which had always felt so homey, where our kids had enjoyed visiting, was worth the trouble.

Top: *The back of the house in Auburn, seen through dogwood blossoms.*
Above Right: *Caroline finding Easter eggs.*
Above: *Loren and Elias sitting on the staircase.*

When I started this remembrance of houses past, I meant to talk about just that, houses, nothing else. But I've discovered that I can't talk about houses without also talking about people and feelings and events and problems and work and play in those houses—everything. Houses are like that. They're central. They may be the outward signs of social distinctions, but their significance goes much further. We express ourselves and what is important to us in how we arrange our houses, the colors we paint the rooms, what we put on the shelves. At the same time, as we go from house to house, in one door and out another, each of them in some way changes us. By the time I reached retirement, the windows of a lifetime of houses had indeed presented what was outside in new ways, and their walls and rooms had helped me examine and re-form my own inner spaces.

PART TWO

Moving into Retirement

CHAPTER FOUR

Deciding to Retire

I T WAS LOREN who started us thinking about retirement. One day in the most casual way, he just dropped the word—the R word—into our conversation, asking innocently enough, "When we retire, what do you think we'll . . ." Or maybe it was, "I was thinking that after we retire, maybe we'll want to . . ." Something like that, something perfectly innocuous.

I nearly snapped his head off. "What are you talking about?" There I was, only in my fifties. I wasn't ready to think about retiring. In fact at that time I didn't think I would ever retire. It simply wasn't in my field of vision. Having come to my profession late and by an unconventional path, and now, contrary to anything I could have expected, having wound up as a tenured full professor, teaching and writing about just the things I wanted to, why would I want to give it up?

Anyway, we both thought of our work as something more than just a job: it was a way of life. One of the deans I worked with during my last administrative years, David Prior, put it best: "This is the only job in the world where you can go on studying whatever it is that interests you the most for as long as you want to and get paid for doing it, on just one condition—that you share what you learn." Exactly.

That's why I was so shocked by Loren's use of the R word. But he is more of a realist than I am. While I was closing my mind and clinging to thoughts of a dramatic obituary—Ninety-Year-Old Professor Dies Mid-Lecture—he was starting to look ahead and think what he did or didn't want to do with the decades of his life beyond sixty-five or so.

Not When But Whether

There is something about merely uttering a word that starts the mind playing with it. Compulsively, even. Once Loren had dropped the word "retirement" into my mind, it stayed. And after only a few months of batting it around, I reached the point where he had started —the realization that even if my work was central to my definition of who I was, and even if I did like it more than any other kind of life I could think of, life wasn't necessarily all work. Along with that came the idea that maybe I might like to explore other possibilities. And I knew that if I was ever going to, I'd better get on with it. From that moment I began to think seriously about retiring.

The next time the subject came up, it was I who raised it, not straight out but indirectly. "Have you ever thought, if you could live anywhere you wanted to, where it would be?"

No, he said, he didn't think he had.

So we began to talk about it at the dinner table, as a kind of game.

That was how we approached the decision to retire—by way of the *where* question, not the *when* question. We left that one alone for a long time. *When* is so unilateral, so unforgiving. You can't go back in time and change your mind. But with *where*, there's more free-dom. Just spread out a map and look: you can go here, or there, or here and then there. Or you can go and then come back, maybe not to the same house, but more or less. Not that we were wanting to move around; we wanted to find the right place, go there, and stay put. But we liked knowing that if we chose badly or if life called us elsewhere, we could go, whereas if we retired early and then wished we hadn't, we couldn't undo it. Time only flows one way. *Where* leaves room for error.

Where

We knew we wouldn't stay where we were. People often say a small college town is the ideal place to retire, and in a sense we were already there. College Station had Texas A&M, and Bryan had a two-year college. But still, they weren't what you think of as college towns. There was little of that small town charm about them. Texas A&M was so huge it made the whole area busy and traffic-bound. It was also, to our eyes, an area of no particular natural beauty. With only a limited number of years left in which to look at the world, we wanted something more to look at.

We also had Doug to think about. After receiving a diploma from the School for the Blind and spending a year at a practical training facility, he had gone to a group home and had gotten a Lighthouse job in San Angelo. It was the belief that he was securely placed there that had empowered me to step out of my first marriage into independence. Unfortunately, the sense of security engendered by that belief was a false one. The group home closed on short notice, leaving us in a lurch. We brought Doug to our house, but couldn't leave him alone while we were at work. So for several weeks I took him to work with me. He sat in my office all day, day after day, sometimes reading Braille books but mostly just being bored, until finally the state school took him back for a year of supplementary training. Now, as we started thinking about retiring, he once again seemed securely placed, this time in Fort Worth, again living in a Lighthouse-owned home and again assembling ballpoint pens in their workshop. So with that confidence we felt free to move wherever we chose. We told ourselves that when we no longer had a work schedule to restrict us, we could visit him more, not less. And of course Doug could fly to one airport as well as another for his holiday visits. Wayne, his social worker, had been putting him on the plane and meeting him when he got back for years.

So we started thinking where it would be.

Up to this point in our lives we had lived wherever we did primarily because of jobs. Now, anticipating a time with no such restriction, we had more freedom to choose. But with freedom comes complication. We had more, not fewer, factors to consider. Besides questions of climate and natural beauty and accessible doctors and airports, we had to think how far we would be from our children and grandchildren. It wasn't an easy decision, and the stakes were high. Our choice would shape how we lived all the remaining years of our lives.

Place—I mean the nature or quality of a place, even more than its location on a map—is more important to some people than to others. To us it seemed very important indeed. We gave a great deal of thought to the kind of place we wanted before we started making a list of possibilities.

We decided right away that we wanted our home for retirement to be located in either a rural or a small-town setting. We could imagine the pleasures of real city life, shops and restaurants within walking distance, concerts a subway stop away. That kind of living sounded wonderful. But it didn't sound like us.

Our second requirement was that the climate be cooler and less humid than in the Brazos Valley of Texas. Of course, almost any place is. And we wanted some winter. We wanted four seasons to the year.

If those two were easy, settling on how we wanted the land around us to look required only slightly more thought. People say that everyone is either a mountain person or a beach person when it comes to vacations. We weren't discussing a vacation spot, of course, but the setting for the next stage of our lives. But if everyone is one or the other, we are definitely mountain people. Loren had liked living with a mountain horizon during his years at Caltech. I had only visited mountains on vacation trips, but remembered how sad I always felt when I started home and the sight of them faded. So we knew we wanted to live within a mountain horizon, or at least within, say, a half-day's drive of one.

Last, we wanted a big sky. I was the one who was especially adamant on this. None of those closed in places for me.

I have a theory about this. I think that for most of us the way the sky looks when we first come to awareness in life is the way the sky ought to look. Logic has nothing to do with it. I had realized just how deeply I felt this when we made our abortive move to Alabama. When I visited for the interview I was struck by what a pretty place it was—dogwoods blooming, tree-covered hillsides, camellia bushes in all the yards. But when we actually moved, my feelings changed. This time we drove rather than flew in, and the closer we got the more it seemed like driving through a long green tunnel. Dense woods on both sides of the highway closed in around us and shut out the sky. Yes, Auburn was a flowery, pretty place. But I just can't live inside a dense tree canopy.

Surprisingly, although Loren grew up in even bigger big-sky country than I did—on the open plains of Nebraska—this feeling about an open sky isn't so deep-seated for him. Still, he does understand what I'm talking about. Or at least, he tolerates it.

We had four criteria, then—rural or small-town, cooler and drier climate, in or near mountains, not too shut in by tree canopy. We felt confident that these were fixed preferences and weren't going to shift. Then for the sake of practicality we added one more: close enough to a city to provide easy access to medical care and an airport. Travel was also an important part of our vision of retirement. So that meant our ideal place couldn't be so very rural, after all.

Ready access to medical care should have been obvious from the start, of course, but it was an older friend who called it to our attention. Before he retired, he said, he imagined a house in the country overlooking a big pasture of cows. But with burgeoning health problems he had come to think a herd of doctors and a good hospital were even better.

We actually made a list of places to consider. And as we did, we adhered to our criteria pretty well, but not entirely. We kept trying to think, for instance, whether there wasn't someplace in Texas we could like for its own sake that would put us reasonably close to Doug as well as to other children and grandchildren.

We considered, for example, the Hill Country, a very popular retirement area lying more or less west of San Antonio and wrapping around the west side of Austin. I had been to Kerrville in the Hill Country once, and had an idea that it had cool evenings even in the middle of summer. So we made a weekend trip to look around. But we just couldn't work up any enthusiasm for it. Even if the temperature did drop at night, it was still a hot climate. We thought, too, of Brenham, a pretty old town set in green hills about halfway between Houston and Austin, with well maintained older houses or pleasant acreages for building. We sent off for real estate brochures and turned through them, but never really pursued the idea. Our hearts were set on something higher and drier. In the same way my thoughts, but not Loren's, turned for a while to the little town of Grandview, south of Fort Worth. I think it was mainly the name that appealed to me; I liked the look of it on the exit sign from the interstate. And I liked the general lay of the land as we drove past the exit on our way to Bryan—gently rolling, with vistas of cotton fields or hay fields sloping up to a gentle ridge or dipping down to a creek lined with brushy trees. It didn't have mountains, of course, but it did have a big sky. I thought it looked very *Texas*. And Grandview would put us close to Doug. But we never so much as turned off at the exit to go see if the town lived up to its name. Truly, it didn't meet our criteria. It wasn't even very convenient to an airport.

I kept asking Loren if he was sure he didn't want to go back to the Sand Hills of Nebraska, back to his roots. He always said no, but I kept worrying that he was just saying that because he thought I didn't want to. I didn't. But after all, he still had family ties there, and I wanted him to get to go home for retirement if he wanted to. No, he said, he had been gone too long, and besides, it's too cold in winter. We didn't speak of it any more.

If we sometimes strayed from our criteria, then, we quickly got back on track.

Here are the places we seriously considered:

Southern Colorado. We had driven through this less populated and less frequented part of Colorado around Trinidad and Walsenburg several times, and we remembered it as being spacious, high and dry, and cool, with nice mountain scenery. I wrote off to the chamber of commerce for information, and we studied it carefully. We liked what we saw. But we were deterred by two considerations. It would be awfully cold in winter; we wanted some winter, yes, but probably not that much. And it seemed maybe *too* far from the city bustle—more specifically, too far from a major airport. Medical resources, we didn't know; we never checked into it. All in all, it seemed like too dramatic a change.

Northern Arizona. People we'd met at my cousin Jeanie's once had remarked that Prescott, Arizona, was the best place in the country to retire. That sounded like a pretty strong endorsement. So on our way home from a spring-break trip to Phoenix we drove through to take a look. It is indeed a scenic area, mountainous, and certainly cooler and drier than central Texas. Prescott itself struck us as a nice sized town, not too big and not too little, and it seemed to have some music and theater available. We again wrote to the chamber of commerce (this was before the day of getting such information on the Internet) and soon started getting brochures. But as we studied them, we began to feel that though it all looked attractive, it just didn't seem right. It didn't seem real, somehow. Everything seemed tailored to what some developer thought retired people wanted, but that wasn't necessarily what we wanted. We saw descriptions of condos, gated communities, and golf courses; we saw pictures of patio home clusters and well-dressed couples dancing on terraces or gazing at sunsets. But we didn't want to live in an enclave of pleasure-seekers all the same age. With apologies to the fine people who live there and love it, we thought Prescott looked synthetic. I don't claim our impression was accurate, just that it was our impression.

West Virginia. We had visited and liked that eastern neck of West Virginia that reaches across Virginia toward Washington—and specifically, Shepherdstown—when we were on research leave in the DC area in the mid-nineties. A friend of mine who taught there at Shepherd College invited us to drive out for dinner and a student play. The restaurant turned out to be well worth the drive, even without the pleasure of spending an evening with a friend, so that was another plus. And the town—the whole area, really—was truly picturesque. Now we gave it some serious thought.

Once again we sent off for real estate brochures. We quickly learned that Shepherdstown itself was out of our price range but that land prices dropped sharply only a few miles farther west, where the beautiful green mountains rose higher. We also learned that there was convenient train access to Washington; it would be entirely feasible, from a perch on one of those ridges, to hop on the train in the morning, spend the day at a museum, and be back home before bedtime—an ideal mix of country and city. Plus, we already knew there was good bluegrass music every Saturday night in a tiny nearby town. And we would have people nearby who loved us and could be counted on to look after us in our dotage—a former student of Loren's and his wife in Potomac, Maryland, and our dear friends Beth and Roy Alvarez in College Park. They were all saying come east, come live near us.

We made a return trip and drove around looking, from the outside, at a few houses and pieces of land we'd seen listed in the brochures. We saw some beautiful home sites that seemed very reasonably priced.

But we couldn't get beyond some downers. First, though Doug didn't seem anxious about our moving away, we felt uneasy about going so far. We'd also be very far from the Texas grandchildren, and we knew they weren't going to be flying up to see us as often as we would wish. But there were other things, too. West Virginia would have put us in mountains, yes, and in a cooler climate, but by no means a drier one. There's a reason for all that beautiful greenery: moisture. It's humid as heck up there. Then there was the tree canopy. The more I saw of that beautiful greenery, the more it closed in on me. It shut out the sky. And basically we didn't think we would ever feel like we belonged there. We are both westerners. We didn't think we would ever be able to feel like easterners. It was the last place to drop off the list.

It's funny, I don't think I had ever, until then, consciously thought of myself as a westerner. I hadn't honestly thought of myself as anything, regionally. Yes, I was from Texas, and Texas was in the South (so I thought of it, more than West). But I just hadn't grown up feeling very strongly defined by region. Even in elementary school I always felt secretly glad that the North had won the Civil War. And any ties of loyalty to region that I'd had to begin with had been further weakened by all the moving around I'd done in my adult years. But now, suddenly, I felt differently about it. I felt a pull of identity toward the West—or more precisely, the Southwest.

Serious thinking about retirement and about place, either of them separately or both together, often does this. It draws a person into thinking about identity in fundamental ways that have been easy to avoid or evade earlier in life.

New Mexico. The last name left on our list, the place where we would find our lot, hadn't even entered the discussion until fairly late. But once it did, it stayed.

WHY THERE?

People kept asking us, Why New Mexico? There was no easy answer. Certainly we didn't have roots there—me from Fort Worth originally, Loren from a cattle ranch in Nebraska. And certainly it wasn't close to our children. At the time we started thinking seriously about the *where* question, there were Lutes kids in Seattle, Austin, Houston, and Arlington (Texas, not Virginia); Stout kids in Houston, Fort Worth, Atlanta, and Cleveland (Ohio, not Texas). The grandchildren were all in Texas. By choosing New Mexico, we were going farther from them all. Angel, the son-in-law with whom we are very close, was deeply hurt by it. But we felt our lives winding down, and it was important to us to spend these years in the right place.

This is how it happened.

Car time has always been talk time in our marriage. By the time of that spring-break car trip when we went through Prescott, we had been talking for months about where to retire. So naturally the topic kept coming up all during the trip. Somewhere along the way, feeling a little weary of our new obsession, we started playing a game of "Spot the Perfect Place." Passing the dreariest, most inhospitable patch of earth you can imagine—a junkyard on the fringe of some unprepossessing town or a stretch of bleak and barren flat land with a weathered For Sale sign stuck up on it—one of us would exclaim, "That's it! That's the Perfect Place!" And we would laugh. But of course the serious undercurrent was still there. We were looking for the perfect place; we just didn't know where it was.

The purpose of the trip was to visit my son Alan and his wife Shanna, who were living in Tempe at the time. After we'd been there a day or two, Doug flew over from DFW and we took him to an Angels spring training game, then drove him back with us. The first day, after leaving Tempe, we looped through Wickenburg and Prescott and Flagstaff and spent a night in Gallup. Doug was startled and delighted by the Navajo language radio broadcasts we picked up that afternoon. The next morning we got an early start and made a visit to Acoma before stopping for a late breakfast at a Denny's in Albuquerque. Then we got back on I-40 and climbed the jagged, pinkish-brown western slope of the Sandia Mountains.

When you pass the crest, the brownness suddenly takes on a tinge of green. This is because the eastern side of the ridge catches more rain and snow than the western side, toward the city. We were traversing the roller-coaster of that greener eastern slope, just a few miles beyond Tijeras Pass, not yet to the Estancia Basin and the slow pull up to the last high ridge and the downward slide into Texas, when I glanced to the left and saw a deep green ridge with a handful of houses scattered across its flank. It stood out distinctly against the sky, with a brown rocky-topped peak beyond it.

"That looks like a good place," I said. "No really," figuring Loren would think I was still playing the game, "I mean it."

Since he was driving, he could only catch a glimpse, but he agreed that it did look nice. I scrambled for pen and paper as an exit sign loomed up and wrote down the name: Edgewood. More rural than urban; a cooler and drier climate, for sure; and not just close to mountains but actually in them. Views all around.

After we got home, I looked up Edgewood in the zip code directory at the post office and sent an inquiry addressed Chamber of Commerce, Edgewood, NM 87015. After a couple of weeks it came back stamped Unknown. I tried again, addressing it City Hall, Edgewood, NM 87015. Again it came back Unknown. At this point it would have been easy to give up, as we had on several other ideas already. But I kept seeing in my mind that green ridge with the jagged mountain beyond it against New Mexico's clear sky. So I tried telephoning. Called information and asked the operator for the Edgewood City Hall. No such listing, she said. (It wasn't even an incorporated town at that point.)

"So what *is* there in Edgewood?" I asked.

"There's a fire station," she said, "and a library."

I chose the library.

The library turned out to be a little volunteer operation open for just a couple of hours twice a week. By good luck, I happened to call during one of those two-hour stretches. Not only that, but the person who answered was friendly. She had just moved there from Texas herself, she said, and she loved it. I asked if she could she give me a couple of names and numbers of real estate agents. Sure she could! And when we went out to the Santa Fe Opera the next summer, we arranged to meet one of them for an exploratory session.

We had gone to Santa Fe for the summer operas before, pulling our tiny pop-up camper and staying at the KOA. Evenings, we changed into our opera duds in the campground shower room and were off. For the summer of 1996, we bought tickets for two nights, back to back. As we planned the trip, we decided to take the back way to Santa Fe, exiting the interstate at Edgewood and cutting north there instead of going into Albuquerque to take I-25. That way, we could get a look at the area to the east of the city before linking up with the real estate agent on our way back.

We were not encouraged by what we saw. NM-344 is down on the flats; it runs along the edge of the dusty Estancia Basin. True, we could see mountains off in the distance, and our list of criteria had only specified being close to mountains, but the houses we passed all seemed to sit in a swirl of blowing dust-on a bare plain with not the least bit of privacy. We fell silent.

After our two nights of opera, we headed south again, but this time by a different route, NM-14, often called the Turquoise Trail. Going down 14 from Santa Fe, we first passed through a noble desolation with a few scattered houses, then climbed ridges and skirted gullies in an intriguing up-and-down world affording glimpses of the Jemez Mountains off to the west, before winding through the old mining town of Madrid. As we went, the sparse dotting of cactus yielded to a sprinkling of junipers, then a mixture of junipers and piñons (the state tree of New Mexico, a squat, short-needled, nut-bearing pine that dominates the woodlands at certain elevations). Our spirits rose. By the time we got into Cedar Crest, where we were meeting the realtor, Diane, we were seeing actual trees and little mountain roads running off every which way.

Cedar Crest itself, it turned out, is pricey. Any lot we could afford there would be significantly smaller than we thought we wanted. (At that point, we were still thinking we might keep a few goats.) Diane, who turned out to be the very person we needed, also thought the difficulties of getting out to the main road in winter from one of those high spots around Cedar Crest might be more than we wanted. I suppose she was thinking of the need for old folks like us to get to the doctor. We didn't yet think of ourselves as old folks, but it was reasonable enough for her to, once the word "retirement" came into play. If we wanted two or more acres, she said, we needed to look a little farther out from the main ridge. So she gave us a kind of orientation tour to help us develop a sense of the possibilities.

It quickly became clear that the five or ten acres we'd had in mind was going to cost entirely too much unless we bought in an area of uncertain water supply. In the absence of a public water system or even one of the private systems scattered across the East Mountains (meaning, the mountains east of Albuquerque), we would have to put in our own well. And in some parts of the area, she said, some otherwise very attractive parts, it was not unusual to drill dry holes. She knew of people who had their water hauled in by truck. We had been saving our money and we felt confident that our retirement annuities were going to meet our needs, but we didn't have the kind of money to be drilling dry holes or buying water by the truckful.

It also became clear as Diane toured us around how greatly the scenic quality varied from spot to spot and how these variations related to the building process. Relatively small distances took us from a ridge top to a narrow valley between ridges, with obvious results for what you can or can't see. Not that all the advantages were one way. A "meadow lot," as she called it, would be relatively free of major rocks and relatively level, thus easier and cheaper to build on, and might afford a splendid view of mountains, but would probably not have trees. A ridge lot, on the other hand, would have juniper and piñon trees, hence more of a sense of hideaway, but was likely to be rocky as well as sloping, thus harder and more expensive to build on. It might or might not afford a view of mountains, since it would be more or less on the mountain that the meadow lot people were looking up at, but if it had views out over the lower expanses it would afford a great sense of space. Loren preferred the ridge lots right off. I was firmly in the middle. At the end of our half-day tour we thanked Diane and drove away, clutching a local weekly newspaper with a cover story of a bear treed right in Cedar Crest. This promised to be exciting!

During the Christmas-New Year break, after we drove Doug back from his Christmas visit, we flew to Albuquerque and did some serious looking. Diane showed us a few houses and some lots, and we drove around some on our own, up onto the slopes of South Mountain itself, the brown peak we had seen beyond the Thunder Mountain ridge, where sleet nearly sent us sliding off the road. We also went south into the Manzanos, where we got into dense long-needled pine forest, very beautiful but not consistent with a big-sky requirement. We wanted a few trees, yes, but we wanted to be able to see out.

Once we saw the lot in Thunder Mountain Estates and stood there and looked out over the valley and looked at each other in that "this just may be it" kind of way, it became the measure by which we considered everything else. But we were determined to look some more. An especially pretty lot we found on our own, south of the interstate, seemed to have everything we wanted, really good views and trees and a lower price than Thunder Mountain, but the more we sat in our car and looked at it, and at a house just down the way that had obviously been under construction for a long time and didn't appear likely ever to be finished, the less we trusted it. Then there were a couple of meadow lots I liked, priced $10,000 less than the Thunder Mountain lot and surely easier to build on, but they were just so bare, and the road they were on looked as though it would be a rutted muddy mess in bad weather. There were also two ridge lots a mile or so in toward the city, that were priced right and had great views, but they were difficult to get to and even rockier and more thickly strewn with cactus than the Thunder Mountain lot. The day turned cold and windy. We stood there on the two rocky lots, going back and forth in our minds, as snow turned to sleet. "I'm not ready to rough it this much," I stated.

We headed for our motel room. The next morning we drove out for one more look at the Thunder Mountain lot before turning in our rental car and flying home. As soon as we got there, we phoned Diane with an offer. The seller countered. We met him halfway.

We had bought ourselves a lot. We didn't realize until much later that Thunder Mountain was the very ridge I had spotted the day we were passing on the interstate with Doug in the back seat.

Once we had bought our land, our faces were set toward retirement, though it would be five more years yet before we went. In the meantime, we planned our house, and at least once a year we went back to look at our two-and-a-half acres of rocks, juniper, piñon, and cactus.

This is what it was like.

The dirt and gravel road ran steeply along the east side of the ridge that developers had christened Thunder Mountain. To the right of the road, going up, the land dropped sharply away to the flats below. To the left it rose toward the central spine. Our lot was on the high side. Every year when we made our annual visit, we parked on that same exposed slab of rock that Diane had parked on when she first brought us to see it, and clambered up again over the embankment made by the grading of the road, and stood looking in all directions. As the Navajo say, "Beauty all around us."

At first, I found it a little frightening. It was so different from any spot of earth I'd ever lived on—bigger, for one thing, as well as more rugged. Then, too, as we rambled around looking for the survey markers at the corners or admiring cactus blooms or wondering what kind of animal had dug the tunnel we found in a rock-free spot about halfway back, we sometimes got lost from each other in the brush. I could have easily lost track of which way to go to get back to the road. Later, of course, I learned the slopes and rocks, clearings and thickets, and then, after we built the house, its roof provided orientation too. But at first I felt uneasy—about getting lost, about falling, about stepping in cactus. Not uneasy about encountering a bear, because at that point I didn't know that bears came onto our ridge. Twice, in fact, they had scratched at window screens at the only house we could see from what was going to be our back door. Uneasy that the dogs we could hear barking—big ones, from the sound of them—might be running loose. Not uneasy about coyotes; I figured they'd run from humans. Dogs won't.

Sure enough, the only time we encountered a coyote during those years it came trotting casually down from the crest of the ridge while Loren was crawling through brush setting pins for some improvised surveying he was doing. Engineers know how to do such things. The instant the coyote saw him, it wheeled around and streaked away.

There were three basic types of cactus to avoid as we walked around: cholla (pronounced *choy-yuh*), a cluster of long, branching arms about two inches thick, reaching up maybe six feet from a common center; prickly pear, the familiar cluster of flat pads with strong thorns; and the kind I call pin cushion cactus, but which I think is really called claret cup—a low dome of rounded nodes thickly covered with fine prickles. Then, too, there was yucca. The sharp points on the end of the yucca's sturdy elongated leaves can penetrate jeans and draw blood. I speak from experience. It was a sharp and spiny land, and if it weren't for the slopes and peaks, and of course the sky, probably not as easy to love as some greener, softer place. I've always tended to prefer plain things. This land was like minimalist art, stark but real.

The soil, the dirt itself, was a light grayish brown that from a distance looked to be tinged with pale orchid or mauve. At first the

Claret cup in bloom.

ground seemed hard, as if nothing could ever be planted in it. But it only *seemed* that way because there are so many rocks. Between the rocks it's actually loose and friable—except when baked hard in mid-summer—loose enough that it readily becomes blowing dust. In winter, when the ground frosts and thaws and gets snowed on and melted into and dried out and frosted and thawed again, it takes on a kind of fluffiness. I don't know how else to describe it. Of course, any soil contracts when it freezes and expands when it thaws and stays that way until it resettles. But it was new to me. It looked unlike any dirt I had ever seen. I'd lived before in places where the ground froze in winter, but they were grassy places, so I didn't notice. A different texture, then, as well as a different palette.

The reason I was so keenly aware of the soil was, of course, the bareness. Clump grasses grow sometimes sparsely, sometimes fairly thickly, depending on the year's rainfall, but either way, patches of bare ground show in between, with a scattering of loose rocks and occasional outcroppings, the earth's bones sticking through its hide. Such grass stays mostly a pale grayish-green. The cactuses, some sticking up above the grass, some hiding down in it, are also a subdued green but in a somewhat yellower shade. At least, you hope so.

The really dangerous bits are the ones that have broken off—some broken by the hooves of deer—and dried up. They turn a gray-brown so close a match to the gray-brown soil or the grayish clump-grass that they're hard to see as you walk through, but their spines still mean business. Then above the level of most of the cactus (not the cholla), the juniper and piñon needles are a darker but harmonizing shade, either a dark yellowish-green or a dark bluish-green, I could never quite decide which. Maybe it varies according to season as well as quality of light.

Junipers and piñons are interdependent; you almost never see one without the other. Usually it's a piñon growing up in the middle of a clump of juniper. Because of their scaly needles, junipers are the more drought tolerant of the two, and thus hardier, and often afford a nurturing bit of shade for a struggling piñon seedling. Everybody prefers the piñons. At first, during our vacation visits, Loren started cutting down junipers in the hope that piñons would take over, but we came to decide that was rather like getting rid of nursemaids in the hope babies will grow up bigger without the interference. So he took to cutting them only if a young piñon seemed to be getting choked or crowded into deformity. On the other hand, juniper is now so much more abundant than it used to be that by competing for water, it weakens the piñon forest. The year we found our land and the years of anticipation were a period of drought when pine bark beetles moved in and many piñons died off. But the seedlings that I saw coming up alongside juniper or in the middle of a clump of cactus seemed to indicate that the piñons weren't going to disappear. Botanists tell us that the piñon-juniper forest has contracted and expanded in cycles for centuries, and I assume it will go on doing so. After a fire or a die-off, the junipers return first, then the piñons.

Every time we were there paying our annual visits, I made it a point to watch for deer droppings. I always felt a certain suspense from one visit to the next that maybe the deer would have decided too many humans (especially Texans) were coming in and would have gone off to someplace more secluded. But if I saw fresh, black droppings I knew the deer were still there. When our granddaughter Melissa went with us a couple of times, she complained that I was always looking at poop. It does sound a little weird when you put it that way. But yes, I was always looking, and was always happy to see black deer poop.

We didn't usually see any actual deer. Once when we went during a Christmas-New Year break and found a heavy blanket of snow all over, busy with tracks, we saw deer standing calmly in a corral down by the front road. Another time, in summer, I scared up a little doe from under some brush and sent her bounding away toward the crest of the ridge. Usually they stayed hidden.

But we never saw a single snake on any of our visits, not even when Loren was crawling around through brush, doing his surveying. Later, when we were building, one of the construction workers found a large bull snake in the garage and escorted it out into the brush. I had a theory that rattlesnakes didn't frequent our elevation (6,800 feet). It was a comforting theory, and I held firmly onto it until a friend whose place was even higher than ours told us he saw them regularly. I admire the respectful attitude toward snakes held by Native American peoples, and I admire the idea of living in harmony with all creatures, pleasant or not, but I hope not to get close enough to Grandfather Snake to extend him even the slightest token of respect, myself. And if I had seen any of the huge centipedes that inhabit New Mexico before we actually packed up and moved there, I might never have gone.

We decided, during those years when we were planning our house and anticipating our move to the high and beautiful, that we would like our patch of earth to have a name. We thought we'd get a nice wooden sign made to put up on the lot. In consideration of its being in New Mexico, we thought the name should be in Spanish. That made the choosing of a name even harder than it usually is, since neither of us is bilingual. We did have sufficient Spanish to think of a few common phrases that would have been suitable enough: Alta Vista, Vista Verde. But we wanted to do better. The challenge of finding just the right name—and we were sure we would recognize the right one when it came along—drove us to buy a Spanish-English dictionary, specifically a Latin American Spanish-English dictionary. It was a considerable help.

I think it was in one of Cormac McCarthy's border books, where he generously intersperses Spanish with his English text, that I had come across the word *cerro*, meaning hill or ridge. It seemed like a good start. But it needed an adjective to go with it. *Cerro Alto*, High Ridge, was too literal. *Cerro Verde*, Green Ridge, was too predictable—even though, after all, it was the deep greenness of that ridge standing up against the sky that had first caught my eye. We kept trying. How we came up with *espinoso* I don't remember. *Espinoso*: spiny, prickly, and also (but we didn't notice this meaning at the time) difficult. *Cerro Espinoso*—Prickly Ridge.

As it turned out, we never had the sign made and rarely used the name in conversation, for the simple reason that I could not learn to say it correctly. Laura, who teaches Spanish, pointed out that the Rs are supposed to be rolled. But that seems to be something I am physically incapable of doing. I still think of our place east of Albuquerque as *Cerro Espinoso*—but with unrolled Rs.

WHEN

It was only after we had done all these other things that we again took up the *when* question. At the time we settled on the date, we were both still three years short of sixty-five.

I had become eager, even impatient to go—probably more so than Loren. It was partly an eagerness to go build the house we had been planning, partly the lure of the place itself, but there was also the fact that my job was wearing me out. Four years earlier, after having declared I was through with administrative work and would spend my full time teaching and writing, I changed my mind when the position of dean of faculties came open. It seemed so perfectly suited to my previous experience I just couldn't resist.

It was a great job, with interesting challenges. It gave me a sense of making real contributions to the university, plus the satisfaction of being the first woman to hold the position. And it meant a big salary boost—which in turn meant a faster build-up of my retirement account. But it was simply wearing me down. It wasn't just the piles and piles of paperwork and the long hours; I was used to those. And it wasn't the fact that I could no longer be in the classroom; I still had graduate students. Not so much the long staff meetings with the provost, though those were bad enough. It was the constant pressure of problems I had very little hope of solving: disillusioning ethics charges, intractable grudges, grievance cases in which there seemed to be no fair settlement, negative tenure decisions that could so easily have gone the other way, dean evaluations that were used as opportunities to settle the score anonymously. One of the worst was the case of a faculty member whose divorce settlement had his retirement fund so stripped he was afraid he'd be eating out of dumpsters if he retired, but his medication had him so confused he wrote formulas on the board in circles, and his prostate cancer was causing him to wet his pants in class so the students were laughing at him. What could I do beyond telling his supervisor to go buy that man some adult diapers and send me the bill? Confronting that kind of thing and having no way to put it right takes a person down fast.

But there was a still more pressing reason why we retired when we did. We had a sense of wanting another adventure in life, and we realized that the matter of physical health probably left us only a limited time for having that adventure.

Loren suffers from rheumatoid arthritis. For a while when we were first married, we feared he would be wheelchair-bound. Now, with good medical care, he had stabilized and even improved. But the disease could turn on him again at any time. So if we wanted to climb up to see cliff dwellings or hike across New Mexico's great caldera, we needed to get on with it. So when I told my boss that I was retiring and word began to get around and people asked me why, I had an answer all prepared: "If you want to have another adventure in life, you don't want to wait too long." With typical ineptness, the student newspaper reported it as, "I am a very adventurous person"—as if I'd said I liked to go bungee jumping.

I wonder how many people feel this way, that they want another adventure in life. How many of us retire because we feel that we've gotten all the marrow we can out of whatever bone it is that we've been chewing, and we want to try chewing a different one before we die? If so, how lucky we are if we have a retirement fund built up that will let us go after another bone while we still have teeth to chew it!

What the concept of *adventure* meant to me, as we made our decision to retire, had nothing to do with daring or sports or transient thrills like bungee jumping. And I knew by then that our retirement adventure wasn't going to mean undertaking some strenuous new endeavor in an exotic place. At one time we had thought of joining the Peace Corps some day, but we were no longer up to that. No, adventure now meant something quieter, something more like discovering my capacity for living by a different rhythm, experiencing dailiness in a new way, exploring the nature of a new place. How observant could I learn to be? How still? Or on a day when I didn't want stillness, how far could I walk? What would I see as I went along? How effectively could I learn new ways of filling time, or of letting time fill me? Things like that began to seem like the real adventures.

I think the reason why those of us lucky enough to have a choice in the matter sometimes choose to retire early is that we want to live more than one life. At bottom, I suppose, we all want to live forever, or would if we could stay at our prime. Failing that, we want to live more than once. And since we know we can't do that either, we try to evade death by living more than one life within a single lifespan. Retirement, if we are very lucky indeed, gives us a chance to do that. A last chance to reinvent ourselves and maybe get it right.

CHAPTER FIVE

Planning Our House

LANNING A HOUSE isn't just a matter of drawing walls and the location of doors and windows on a piece of paper or a computer screen. These basics are important, of course, as are floor coverings and paint colors and all the other things that go into making a house, and any botched choice along the way will be a disappointment for a very long time. But a house is more than that. It reflects who we are, shapes who we are. We move from house to house, repainting here, remodeling there, fixing up or scarring up, mowing or littering, and as we do, we remodel ourselves.

Planning a house means planning a life. But that's not easy to do when the house you are planning is for retirement and you haven't yet lived retired. We were trying to guess how our time would be spent in a future of days we were only beginning to imagine. It was entirely different from any of the home looking and home buying we had done in the past. Not only was it harder to plan from the ground up, but we had to give more thought to our personal values and think about our wishes for the future more carefully.

FLOOR PLANS

Rationalists that we are, we went about planning our house in much same way we had gone about deciding where we wanted to live: we first defined a set of basic requirements as guidelines. It must be a single-story house; arthritic knees don't enjoy stairs. It must have three bedrooms, so we could sleep children and grandchildren who came to visit, provided they didn't all come at once. Accommodating these visitors also meant two dining areas, which we wanted anyway because that's what we were used to. There had to be two good work places for desks and computers. A tub and a shower in the master bath. And no matter what, it had to have lots of windows, both for looking out and to provide ventilation. We wanted to live without air conditioning on our mountain ridge. It needed a kitchen big enough that we could work in it together and it needed a variety of comfortable spaces for us to sit together and talk—or sit alone and read or just reflect.

Governing everything else was an assumption that in building this house we would not be trading up but down. In choosing to retire we were choosing to reduce our incomes. We weren't going to be on Social Security alone; we would also have the retirement annuities we (and our employers) had been paying into for years. But the two together would be less than the salaries we'd been getting, and we expected to live accordingly. We weren't exactly planning something on the order of Thoreau's cabin in the woods, but we did expect to observe Thoreau's principle of "simplify, simplify." We would build, we thought, a house of about 1,200 square feet.

At first Loren had his heart set on a log house. Whatever we built, he meant to do part of the work himself, and he knew there were kits available with pre-cut logs and the other basic materials needed for model number so-and-so. He was actually thinking he could put one up all by himself. I think in his heart of hearts that was what he truly wanted to do: build a log house with no help from anybody except for the detailed finish work that requires special skills and the things like plumbing and wiring that have to be done by licensed journeymen in order to pass inspection. I suggested that we might be able to persuade our sons and son-in-law (the aptly-named Angel) to come out and work on it during summer vacations, but he said no, he wouldn't want to impose on them. Anyway, he thought he could rig up hoists to get even the heaviest logs into place without help.

So we got magazines and brochures about log homes and started studying them. I quickly became disenchanted. For one thing, the plans we saw all seemed to run to extremes—either plain little cabins, closer to Thoreau's than we cared to go, or else elaborate multi-level dream homes whose cost would soar along with their soaring vaults. We could never seem to find anything in the middle. Also, in none of the color pictures did the interiors ever look light and bright, and I figured their natural wood tones would only get darker over time. Loren suggested whitewashing, but I remained dubious. Then he saw something in the brochures that even gave him pause. Yearly treatments, inside and out, were recommended to keep the logs sound. Whoa, there! A high-maintenance home was not at all what we wanted for our golden years.

In the end, it was another factor entirely that proved decisive, the same factor that would prove decisive in resolving our uncertainty as to the *when* question: Loren's rheumatoid arthritis. Under attentive care by a series of rheumatologists, it had been stabilized for several years, but now it seemed to go into a new phase. Pain in muscles and joints worsened, swelling and stiffness increased, and his doctor warned him to avoid high-impact activities like hammering. There was no way he could build a house by himself. And with that realization his wish for a log house evaporated.

Now we started collecting books of conventional house plans. We spent hours poring over them. Once again, some that we saw were so elaborate—even fanciful—that I couldn't imagine anyone would ever build them. But some were quite practical. Our books of plans began to bristle with strips of yellow sticky-notes marking pages we wanted to come back to.

Looking at floor plans became our main recreational activity. Not that we had many recreational activities. For years our pattern had been to work late, then rush home to make a simple dinner, clean up the kitchen, do a crossword puzzle together, and then work at our computers some more until bedtime. My taking on the dean of faculties job, with its many evening functions to attend, had squeezed our leisure time down even further. Now house plans took precedence over puzzles and Friday movies. Envisioning our house was central to envisioning our lives in retirement, and we had to do that before we could set the date.

It didn't take long for us to realize that we weren't going to be able to fit all our requirements into the 1,200-square-foot house we'd had in mind—let alone to find a stock plan arranged the way we wanted, with the utility room close to the bedrooms (where most of the dirty clothes come from) and big porches both front and back. If there's any place good for sitting outside it's the highlands of New Mexico, but only if you have shade—so one porch for morning and one for afternoon.

I believe one of the principles of Keynesian economics is that human wants are unlimited. It's a principle I've always objected to, implying as it does an innate and incorrigible greed in human nature, but one I can't claim to have disproved in my own life. So it was with our house planning. One thing led to another, and wants became needs.

Partly it was that there were so many plans, in so many books. Looking at them brought to mind things we hadn't even thought of. And we could so easily compare one with another. All we had to do was turn a page and there was the proof that bigger was better. I don't mean the huge, far-fetched mansions; those never tempted us. But how were we going to fit the piano into one of those tiny living rooms? And the kitchen, now that was going to be important when we were eating in more often. We tried to control the overall size by planning dual-use spaces, but if one of the spare bedrooms was going to double as a study it certainly had to be bigger than the ten by ten cubicles the smaller plans showed. So it went. Our goal for how many square feet kept increasing.

We never found the one right plan that would satisfy all our requirements. If the utility room was where we wanted it, we didn't like the kitchen or there would be only a little porch. But there was one we kept coming back to, one in particular among the two or three with yellow sticky notes still marking the pages after all the others had been taken off and tossed. At 1,700 square feet, it was smaller than we now thought we needed, but we liked the layout and we liked the elevation. Well, no, not entirely; those dormers would have to go; dormers are not plain and functional. But we liked its porch across the entire front and its windows balanced on each side of the front door. So finally, in spite of the $800 or so price tag, we ordered a complete set of plans, knowing full well that we weren't going to build by them. They would give us something to work from.

With not one hour of architectural training but long years as a professor of civil engineering and enormous stores of practical savvy from having grown up on a ranch, Loren meticulously transferred the floor plan to his computer. Then we began to customize. Windows: there had to be two in every room, for cross-ventilation and for light and for enjoying the views. And ceiling fans: one in every room. The master bedroom needed to be bigger; this one would never hold our corner desk arrangement, and we certainly couldn't do without it. So he stretched the whole master bedroom wing by four feet to give room for separate walk-in closets. Then he threw out the bathroom design altogether and redrew it with a bigger shower and a toilet room with a door on it.

So it went. Our ideas grew and so did our floor plan. When it seemed about right, I measured all the pieces of furniture we expected to take with us and made cardboard cut-outs by the same scale as the house plan, one quarter inch equals a foot, and we experimented with furniture arrangements. We could then assess what was going to work and what wasn't and add or adjust spaces, or move doors or windows, accordingly. We found, for example, that once we had added built-in cabinets beside the fireplace, our nice big living room was too small. Of course, stretching the living room, in the middle of the house, front to back, meant stretching whatever was on the other side of the wall from it, the kitchen on one side and the front

guestroom on the other. With the help of the furniture models, we
ascertained that the nice breakfast room, with its bay window overlooking the patio, wasn't going to accommodate our five-foot
butcher-block table. We certainly weren't going to part with that!
Adding a foot to the breakfast room meant making the garage a foot
wider, but after all, you can't have too big a garage. And placing the
cardboard desk and side shelf on the plan for the back guestroom,
where Loren was to have his study, showed that it was also too
skimpy. We added another foot which we later realized should have
been two feet.

That left the matter of a study for me. The plan we had bought
had nothing at all that would do. So now, partly by carving out a

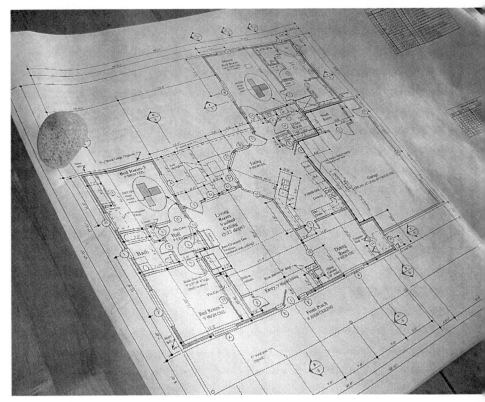

Our house plans.

couple of feet from the garage and partly by adding a little set-off to the dining room wall, Loren designed a kind of closet or alcove to hold my computer desk and side table. This meant redesigning the roof, but so it goes, one thing leads to another, and by this point he was getting good at it. He also gave my study-closet a window so I could see out as I worked—very important—and folding doors to close off the clutter when company came. When they were open for work, the dining table at my back would be handy for spreading out papers. The principle of multi-use spaces in action!

In the end, our simple home for retirement was nothing like the modest cottage we had first imagined. At 2,150 square feet, it was nearly as large as the house we had in Bryan. We felt sheepish. But later, after living in it, we were glad. Yes, our needs and desires simplified with retirement, but at the same time, changes in the way we use a house made the extra space even more important than we imagined. We hadn't fully recognized what giving up our campus offices would mean. Having our offices at home rather than at the campus meant that we needed space not only for desks but for accessible storage of files and books. Even lessons as simple as this take experience to learn. In succumbing to the lure of extra square feet, we lucked out.

Of course, whether a house is big or small, extravagant or modest, is partly in the mind of the beholder. Some of our friends and family, when we showed them our floor plan, said "Wow! That's a big house!" Others, looking at the same plan, asked "Why so small?" We are keenly aware how fortunate we are. We live in a house many people would find palatial. The truly advantaged few would definitely find it skimpy. But so what if they did.

Houses, I say again, are important. They shape not only our daily living but even, I think, our vision of our lives. On the other hand, as we saw from our own behavior while planning and anticipating this house for retirement, it's easy to become overly preoccupied with it. We might have deplored the buy-buy-buy, more-more-more men-

tality we saw all around us, but we didn't always resist it. There's a
slippery slope to traverse from recognizing the importance of a house
for making life comfortable to thinking life can't possibly be good
unless the house is just so.

CHOICES

Besides developing the floor plan, we got involved in a seemingly
endless number of lesser decisions as we planned our retirement
home. These are all necessary, when building, not just for purposes
of "decorating" but so they can be spelled out in the specifications
that the builder will work from—which are also, of course, the basis
for a price quote. We spent untold hours prowling the home stores
and thinking about things like:

Pitch of Roof. A steep metal roof, yes, but how steep? And should
the front porch roof be shed type (a separate pitch slanting out from
the main roof) or a straight continuation of it? Finally Loren built a
scale model of the house with detachable versions of the roof both
ways, so we could step back and consider which we liked better. We
could also look in through the tiny windows of the model to assess
sight lines or remove both roof and ceiling to gaze down into every
room and ponder the relationships of spaces.

Plumbing Fixtures. We didn't care about having fancy toilets, so
we didn't have to look at all the different styles of those, but sinks
seemed like a matter of concern. It's amazing how many sinks the
home stores have to offer. Besides the different materials, there are
so many styles! For kitchens, there are two-compartment, three-
compartment, one-compartment, and variant shapes of all three. For
bathrooms, an array of shapes and colors and decoratively painted
lines—Mickey Mouse, elaborate florals—as well as things that aren't
actually sinks at all but thick glass bowls looming up from low counters. For a while there, I really got into sinks. But in the end we
agreed on good, simple enameled cast iron, off-white.

Faucet Handles, etc. Not to mention shapes and styles, there are choices of faucets in chrome, brass, antique brass, brushed chrome, brushed nickel. The more we looked, the more significant these options seemed. Were we chrome kinds of people at heart or antique brass kinds of people? It began to seem as if something really important were at stake. Certainly there were major differences of price. We decided to plan on brushed nickel and worry about specifics later.

Kitchen Cabinets. With the help of the mock-ups in the home stores, we easily settled on natural maple cabinets in a good, plain style, and felt—wrongly, it turned out—that we'd been careful shoppers.

Countertops. According to *Consumer Reports,* there is no such thing as a perfect countertop material, with no drawbacks. So we decided to stay with simple laminate, preferring the devil we knew to fancier devils we had scarcely met. Besides, it was an economical choice. I collected color samples, laid them out for comparison, held them up against the maple cabinets in the showrooms. Should it blend in or be a contrast, to provide accent? A deep-toned countertop might add interest, but wouldn't it darken the room? But maybe that was a good thing considering New Mexico's intense light. In the end, we chose a dark green similar to the green of our bedroom walls.

There was never any doubt that the bedroom would be a dark, subdued green. We had had dark green walls in our bedroom for the past ten years, ever since the Auburn house. I love green. I was not surprised to learn recently that Muslims consider it sacred.

Actually, I just love color, in itself, in all its nuances. I think of Toni Morrison's wonderful novel *Beloved,* when the dying Baby Suggs gives herself over to pure color. "Bring a little lavender in, if you got any," she calls, "pink, if you don't." I can relate to that. When choosing colors for a quilt, for example, just as with music, I can go off into states of total immersion in color, dissolve into it and lose track of time. And after all, planning a house is somewhat like quilting. You choose among textures and shades, you put the pieces together, you savor the combinations, and then finally you feel satisfaction in the whole quilt, the whole house.

Another consideration was, of course, price. We thought about the dollars a lot. We had lived fairly frugally throughout our marriage and had been pleasantly surprised at how our savings mounted up. We believed we could build for cash, not have a mortgage at all. At the same time, we didn't want to strip ourselves of resources. There would presumably be a lot of living to pay for yet.

All during those years of planning, we kept re-examining our finances. We got estimates of what our annuities would pay if we chose this option or that option; we debated whether to start drawing Social Security at sixty-two, at a reduced rate, or wait until sixty-five, to get the full amount. I did elaborate annual analyses of our expenses, trying to project how our needs in each category would change in retirement (fewer clothes, more travel, less eating out). It looked as though we were going to be OK, but we knew we'd better not shave our safety margin too close. Every decision became a financial decision. What were brushed-nickel faucets going to do to our reserve?

Fortunately, during those years of anticipation we were also given to thinking about things that didn't cost a dime. Things like how much we were going to enjoy keeping windows open in the cooler climate of New Mexico (something rarely feasible in Texas) and how fine it would be, with the windows open, to hear coyotes howling as we lay in bed before sleep. How rain would sound on the metal roof. How nice it would be to sit out on the porch and read. And indeed after we moved into our wonderful house I went on a Dickens spree, re-reading all the ones I'd read years before plus a couple I hadn't, and we both re-read all the Tony Hillerman mysteries. What a great way to spend retirement—sitting by the window or out on the porch, reading Dickens, reading Hillerman.

When

Even while we were planning the house, we kept kept putting off the *when* question. It hovered in the background for years, emerging now and then only to be shoved back again. From the day we bought our land, we were eager to get on with it, to get there and live in the circle of New Mexico's wonderful horizon instead of just visit it once or twice a year. Yet we knew it was too soon; we weren't sixty yet when we started all this. When the right time would be, we didn't know.

For a while we toyed with the idea of retiring on the last day of the twentieth century. It had a certain dramatic appeal. But that would mean, technically, the last day of 1999, much too soon after my acceptance of the dean of faculties job. Then Loren took on an administrative role in his department and also decided he wanted to produce at least one more Ph.D. student before leaving. So we kept waiting—until the summer of 2001, when suddenly the balance tilted and we knew we were ready to decide. We turned in our letters.

So 9/11 played no role in the decision. We had already named the date before that awful day. But it had an enormous effect on how we felt about our last months at the university and even how we felt about retiring.

Like many others, I remember exactly where I was and what I was doing when I heard the news that morning. I had dropped Loren off near his building, on the other side of the campus, and was near my parking garage when I heard on NPR that a small plane had crashed into the World Trade Center. How strange! I thought. But at that moment I lost radio signal as I cleared the gate and went down the short ramp and around the regular, everyday turn to my assigned space. I turned off the ignition, walked out of the garage and across to Rudder Tower, and took the elevator up to the eighth floor to drop off my bag and look over a couple of things before going down one floor to the provost's 8:30 staff meeting. When I gathered up my agenda and pen and went to the elevator, I was no longer thinking about the small plane that had hit that much taller tower fifteen hundred miles away. It was only when I arrived at the conference room that I learned what had really hit the World Trade Center— and our country, and the lives of us all.

I remember sitting at that conference table with the others who sat there every week—except that our boss was now stranded in California—discussing, first, whether to cancel classes. We decided it would be better to try to hold the students on campus. We suffered enough mayhem on the highways every weekend without turning forty thousand students out in their cars all at once to become *more* 9/11 casualties. All morning, it was one question like that after another. We periodically adjourned to the next room, where there was a TV, to stare at the screen as bodies hurtled down and buildings collapsed, then went back to the conference room to field more questions. The head of the Galveston campus had decided in the first few minutes to impose as close to a lock-down as possible, and now he kept calling in to report on how it was going. Galveston is connected to the mainland by a single narrow causeway. If the students started pouring across it, they would be heading straight toward the petrochemical complex around Texas City. At that point, we had a real fear that more was coming, that a sequence of infernos was going to bloom all across the continent, from east to west. If so, the Texas City plants would be a likely target, and our students, driving close alongside them, might be incinerated. I can't recall a more solemn moment in my entire work life than when we considered that danger. I think I continued to feel the strain of it through all the rest of my days at the university.

Texas A&M had already had one disaster during my time as dean. In November 1999 the collapse of the annual bonfire had killed twelve students and maimed more than twice that many. For days afterward I went from meeting to meeting leaking tears. It was as if the spigot would not be turned off. At first, when people noticed and asked me if I was OK, I felt embarrassed. Later I decided, damn it, it was high time they saw their administrators cry! And then, not two years later, came this vastly worse disaster.

After that, the date we had circled on our calendar seemed almost incidental. There were far more momentous things to think about than this or that month, this or that year. And for the rest of the time until January 31, 2002, in that newly post-9/11 world, there wasn't a day at work or away from it when the strain wasn't ratcheted up several notches. It depleted me all the faster than the work, by itself, would have. When retirement day came, I felt even more worn down, even more ready to get away from the pressure and the hectic schedule.

What an innocent time the pre-9/11 summer of 2001 seems now! But at the time, not knowing what was coming, all we were thinking of was the big event waiting beyond our personal horizon, after January. It seemed time, then, to set the process in motion so the actual building of the house could start the minute we arrived—but not a minute before! We meant to be there to see it all. We had chosen a builder—a husband and wife team—a couple of years before. So now, planning our usual little car trip to Colorado with Doug, we decided to swing by the East Mountains and meet with them. After all the planning we'd done, we thought we were ready.

Choosing a builder is largely, I think, an act of faith. It hadn't been easy. We had started with some suggestions from Diane and interviewed four the summer after we bought our land. We had chosen Ray and Joyce (not their real names) basically because we thought their cost-plus method of working made sense and we liked their straightforward manner. "We build Chevies, not Cadillacs," they had said. We liked that. So we said we wanted them to build our house and we e-mailed them whenever we had questions. When the plans were far enough along, we stopped by on one of our trips to Colorado pulling the camper, and they shook Doug's hand and poured him some coffee and he listened in. We didn't realize how much he really enjoyed it until later, when he started chortling over being in on a "business meeting." He had liked being included, simple as that. So we were glad he was going to be along on this meeting too.

In the meantime, Ray and Joyce had beaten us to it; they'd retired themselves and were turning over their business to their construction foreman (let's call him Buddy). So, when we stopped on our way to Colorado that day, we met with all three. Ray and Joyce generously invited us to meet at their house, over coffee, to go over things. Actually, I think we were Buddy's first customers, and they were trying to help him learn the ropes.

While we occupied ourselves with coffee and homemade coffee-cake there at their dining table, the three of them, Ray and Joyce and Buddy, studied our plans. From time to time they nudged each other and silently pointed at something. Then the talking began. Joyce had several questions. She thought the second bathroom was incorrectly arranged, that it wouldn't suit people's expectations for what should be where. Loren explained why he had done it that way—so the toilet wouldn't be visible from the living room. But it wouldn't be, she insisted; the sink cabinet would block it. We said we would think about it. She suggested a skylight in the utility room, and led me off to see hers. We drew in the skylight. And a bigger pantry, she said. Winter weather could be bad in the East Mountains, and we would want to be able to store plenty of food just in case. Bigger pantry, check. Ray asked if we didn't want to make everything wheelchair accessible, but we said no, we didn't. Loren had come all too close to needing a wheelchair long years before, and it was a possibility we weren't ready to think about again.

We had supposed this meeting would last until maybe noon. Instead, at noon all of us but Joyce went out for burgers and stopped by the lot, which Buddy hadn't yet seen. For half an hour or so we tramped around looking at slopes, at rockiness, at where the utility lines would come in. It was not easy for Doug, what with the rough terrain and all the cactus. Everything began to seem more and more complicated. But they professed themselves satisfied, and we went back to the house.

At that point the spec sheet came out, the list of specifications a builder has to get before working up a cost estimate. We had thought, with all our trips to the home stores, we were prepared for this moment, but until we confronted the spec sheet we had no idea how many choices there would be. Certainly we hadn't known they would all be thrown at us at once.

For the stucco exterior, did we want sand finish? We had no idea. For the inside frames of windows, did we want wood all around or only at the bottom or no wood at all? On openings that weren't to be closed off with doors, did we or didn't we want wooden casements? Did we want brass, antique brass, or chrome faucets? (There we had them—brushed nickel, which wasn't even on their list.) Did we want a traditional silver metal roof or a green one? Green would cost more. We said we'd think about it. On and on like that, for five legal-size pages, until we began to realize that like the knight in the Monty Python movie who, when asked his favorite color, says "red—no, blue! blue!" we had not only pulled answers out of thin air when in fact we didn't know but had actually given answers that didn't reflect our real preferences. We asked if we could just take a fresh checklist with us and fill it out when we got home. They shrugged. Sure.

It was about five o'clock when at last we hit the road, knowing we wouldn't get anywhere near as far as we had planned to go before stopping for the night. All of us utterly drained by the long day, we drove along in silence for at least half an hour. Then Doug piped up from in back, "This is going to be the best house ever!" With that, he was glad to lie across the seat and take a little snooze.

Loren asked if I thought Joyce was right about the arrangement of the hall bath.

I thought how competent she seemed, how attentive to details, how sure of herself.

"Yeah," I said. "I think she is."

When we got home, he redid the bathroom layout in his computer. We never revisited the issue, never put a ruler to the plans to
check the sight line or looked through the windows of our house
model. And guess what? The toilet was visible from the end of the
living room.

CHAPTER SIX

Leaving

RETIRING MEANS LEAVING. Most obviously, leaving your job, but also leaving the people you see every day. You also leave a pattern of life that has structured your time and energies for a long time, maybe a whole adult lifetime. You leave that pattern without knowing whether you can find another one to replace it. For some, retiring may mean leaving a sense of personal importance and wondering whether you will ever feel so important again. So it takes some courage to retire. It's a leap into the unknown, and the unknown is always a little bit scary.

For those of us who have decided to leave in a geographical sense, by going to live somewhere else, retiring also means leaving a familiar place—streets we know how to navigate, the grocery store that has a good deli counter, the tree in the park where we've picked up pecans every fall. That, and more, is what moving to New Mexico for our retirement years meant for Loren and me—leaving on top of leaving. Our retirement meant leaving the house where we'd lived for most of our married years. It meant leaving children and grand-children who lived a mere hundred miles away. For me, it meant leaving the state where I was born. Leaving our doctors and our dentist. We left pieces of furniture that we had sold in our two garage sales and temporarily left most of the rest, because our realtor had said we shouldn't empty out the house because it would show better with furniture in it. We left our mower and edger—no more mowing for us! (We have since bought a new mower and a new edger.) We left my mother's china cabinet and the dining room chairs with covers she had needle-pointed herself—gave them to Alan and Shanna for their house in Houston. Mahogany and needlepoint didn't fit into our plans for our rugged new life. Eager to enter the new phase in our life together, we left the only kind of life we had known.

SAYING GOOD-BYE

On Thursday, January 31, 2002, about five o'clock, I walked out of my office for the last time carrying a last box of odds and ends, and drove around to the other side of the campus to pick up Loren. He had officially retired two weeks earlier but had kept coming to the office to clear things out. On this last day, he had several more boxes of papers to load into the car and take home.

Like Loren, I had spent many hours, in the weeks leading up to this day, going through my accumulation of teaching notes, exams, term papers, grade sheets, and files of research materials. Both of us had journals and books galore—more, certainly, than we wanted to haul with us to New Mexico. And we both wound up bringing home from our offices carloads of stuff we couldn't bear to throw away. We knew we had probably tossed out things we would wish we hadn't and boxed up things we might as well have tossed.

He had retired at the end of a semester, as professors usually do. My choice of retirement date had been governed by a different calendar—the yearly schedule of faculty personnel decisions. Just like every other year since I'd been in the office, the year's promotion and tenure files had arrived from all around campus just after the fall commencement. I had studied the cases—some eighty of them—over the holiday break and had spent much of January meeting with the deans to discuss them. On the morning of my retirement day, the provost and I met with the president to review the cases. I felt good knowing that I was working right up to the end.

That afternoon there was a reception, one of those occasions when gifts are presented and speeches are made.

Actually, this was the second reception in honor of my retirement. The first had been given just before Christmas by the organization of women faculty. As the crowd dwindled at the end of the stated two hours, after refreshments and chats and hugs and a formal presentation of a gift (computer software for studying the night skies), a woman I didn't recognize walked up, looked me in the eye, and said her name—just her name, nothing else—and I knew immediately who she was and why she was there. Her tenure case had come up the previous year, in a close decision that seemed to me to be going the wrong way, and I had fought hard for her. We looked at each other and held hands for a minute, knowing what a strong bond we shared. I think it is not too much to say that in her eyes, I had saved her career. But what she had meant to me was at least as precious— the privilege of getting justice done. How lucky I was to have had a job in which, even if only in a few instances, I could make a difference in people's lives! Out of sixty-eight years of living (sixty-eight and counting), it is moments like this that will stay stars in the dark of forgetting.

The reception on my retirement day was campus-wide. The entire faculty was invited. Just as I was about to leave my office and walk down to the reception hall, a young professor from our statistics department, a dear and gentle young woman so brilliant she was always being courted by other universities, came to present me a box of chocolates as a farewell gift. In her somewhat halting English she said that she wouldn't be able to attend the reception, but wanted to tell me that she had treasured my presence and wished I weren't going. I could tell by her expression that she meant it. But to me, *she* was the treasure. I had to turn my back to shut off the tears, knowing that once they got started there would be no stopping them. I hope she understood. (Naisyin, I do miss you.)

For four years my work had brought me into some degree of contact with most of our two thousand-plus faculty members. Now what seemed like a throng of well-wishers crowded around, clutched my hands, and hugged me. During the formal presentation, nice things were said that I wish I could recall. I remember being hugged by the president in front of the whole assembly. But the standout memory of all is of the associate dean of one of the colleges, a terse, crusty sort of guy, with whom I'd worked on a variety of issues. He came through the line, said good-bye, and turned away in tears. I was astonished.

We knew we were going to miss our circle of friends at Texas A&M and wondered if we would be able to make new ones. Without the routine contacts provided by a work life, it was probably going to be harder to meet people, and neither of us is exactly scintillating, socially. We're quiet, we stay home and work on our research, we have trouble thinking of anything to say at parties. We wondered if we would be lonely. It was a real and serious question.

Of course, we had fallen in love with a landscape. But it seems to me that if you don't have that kind of compelling reason, it would probably be best to stay where you are when you retire. Alternatively, it would be a good idea to make one's last move *before* retirement, so as to form new friendships within the social structure of the job.

In fact we had earlier thought about trying to do just that—make a career move to another university in a location we found appealing. But it isn't as easy as it may sound. You can't just phone up and say "please hire me—oh, and also my spouse." What that amounts to is saying, please decide you want to make a couple of hires at the senior level in our two specialty areas (that is, not just in English and in civil engineering but in our specialty areas within those departments), as opposed to any other areas in which you might like to add faculty, and after you have decided you want to do that, please manage to find money in your budget for those positions, and please choose us over all other possible candidates. No, it wasn't going to happen that way. If we were going to reach our place of heart's desire, we were going to have to retire first and then just go and hope we could find some friends when we got there. We also had to hope that our children and grandchildren would come to see us, and that we wouldn't miss them so much between visits that we wouldn't be able to enjoy the new life we were entering.

Maybe, we thought, we would start going to church again, and find friends that way. It had been years since we attended church, and this didn't seem like quite the right reason to go, but we told ourselves that churches serve many needs, and the need for community is one.

This thinking about retirement is a complicated and difficult matter—so many unknowns and no way to know how they're going to work out until we try.

On Friday, February 1, my first day as a retiree, we hauled two carloads of stuff left over from our garage sales to a charity thrift shop. That afternoon we rented a truck and drove it by the furniture store to pick up a new mattress set (since we needed to leave our bed in place for showing the house). I applauded Loren's finesse in backing the truck up our steep and curving driveway. Then we got a few things loaded before showering and dressing for the going-away party at my boss's house.

The provost's office had a reputation for throwing really great going-away parties, and this was no exception. There was a lively crowd, there were great things to eat and drink, and they put on a funny roast based on Johnny Carson's Karnak shtik from the old *Tonight Show*. I had to wear a huge pink satin turban, hold 3x5 cards up to my forehead, and try to come up with publicity slogans for fake book titles that were takeoffs on classics of American literature—a nod toward my teaching field. What smart, witty people, to think up such a thing! Laughs were mixed with the good-byes that night.

HITTING THE ROAD

On Saturday morning, my second day retired, we finished loading up the essentials we were taking along to see us through the construction period on the house, and in the middle of the afternoon, pulled out of the driveway. Loren was in the rental truck, I was in one of the cars. We both stopped and looked back at the home we had so enjoyed, now with a "For Sale" sign in the yard. If neither of us felt particularly sad at that moment, I suppose it was largely because we hadn't raised our children there. So the house we were leaving didn't hold memories like bringing the baby home from the hospital or taking pictures before the prom. It's the memories tied up with children, I think, that make it hard to leave a place. But another reason we didn't shed any tears that day was that we were both so full of anticipation for our new life in the high and dry—the sense of adventure I had cited when my boss asked me why I wanted to retire so early. We had a house to build and a new life to start.

Besides building a house in a new place, the adventure we were embarking on was a change of life pattern—the adventure of finding out whether we could succeed in learning to live by a different rhythm, without offices, without easily measurable goals, without an externally imposed structure for the days, and with less money coming in. As we pulled out, though, this major adventure was taking a back seat in both our minds to the fact of not really knowing where we were going to be living for the next few months. All we had was an address and a signed lease. We had rented the place sight unseen. Nearly all we knew of it was what we were paying and that Loren's son David and his wife Angi (now, to our delight, living in Albuquerque) had looked at it for us and pronounced it "weird but OK." Hitting the road with even just part of your belongings takes on a special edge when you don't know what kind of place you're going to be unloading them into.

This is what we took with us in the truck when we set out for the unknown:

- the new mattress and box springs, with the free frame that came with them;
- two computers;
- one computer desk;

- the wrought iron patio table and chairs, to be used indoors for the interim;
- our very old TV, VCR, and stereo, plus some boxes of videotapes and CDs;
- two canvas camp chairs, to serve as living room furniture;
- an old quilt made by my paternal grandmother, to serve as a bedspread;
- books. boxes and boxes of books; you never know which one you may have an urgent need for;
- the sterling silver in its chest, lest it get stolen while we weren't nearby to guard it; and
- my mother's china.

We didn't get very far that first day. After stopping in Fort Worth to take Doug out for hamburgers, we drove on some thirty miles farther to spend the night at my cousin Jeanie's.

It's strange to me how few relatives I have, beyond my brother, twelve years younger and a world removed in interests and politics. There were four in my father's family, all boys, but none of them had children, so there are no cousins on that side. My mother came from a family of eight, *all* of whom had children, but they were never a close family, so even though there were lots of cousins on that side, I never really knew them. Jeanie and I grew up within ten miles of each other but had never even met until she came to my mother's funeral. Now we talk on the phone, we exchange emails, and sometimes we have falling-outs—like real family members.

After a good night's sleep and a leisurely breakfast with Jeanie and Bud, we felt almost human again and got back on the road. Our goal was Amarillo—not a full day's drive, but it was Super Bowl Sunday and we wanted to stop early to watch the game. We had agreed to stop at every rest area we came to in order to avoid getting separated—which would have been a real problem, with no cell phones (we had never had one) and no motel reservation. Staying together didn't turn out to be hard, but we held to our plan and stopped at every one. It was a cold windy day. The toilet seats in those unheated facilities were a shock every time.

Shortly before Amarillo we started seeing dirty snow left from a big winter storm that had come through the previous week. Snow was something we had seen very little of in our twenty-year marriage. Our weather ordeals had mostly been heat, humidity, and torrential rains. Now the sight of snow gave a certain reality to our sense that we were making a big move, going someplace completely different. It was late when we arrived and got checked in at a motel. The parking lot was so treacherous with melted and refrozen snow that we held onto each other and walked *very* carefully when we went across to the place next door to eat before settling in for the game. If we hadn't driven very far that day, who cared? Why should we hurry? We were retired.

On February 4, using a map Loren had printed off the Internet, we exited I-40 at New Mexico Highway 14, turned up a steep, narrow road—too steep and winding for moving vans, the agent had told us, but only *after* we paid our deposit—and made our uneasy arrival at the sight-unseen house. Loren backed the truck into the driveway, I pulled in after him, and he tramped around to the back through a foot of snow to find the key where the agent had left it. I waited beside the car, feeling tentative.

The house looked pretty good from the outside. It was angular and distinctively shaped, with a walled patio beside the driveway. And it had terrific mountain views to the south and west. But the inside turned out to be something else. It was indeed weird. The arrangement of rooms was so counter-intuitive that we would start for the kitchen with a box of stuff and wind up in a bedroom. There were steps everywhere—up two here, down one there, even a couple of steps midway down the hall, besides a flight with a landing up to the master bedroom. It was a little spooky. And the whole house was off level. We figured the foundation must have a major break somewhere. Just crossing a room, we could feel ourselves walking uphill and downhill. We knew before we even finished unloading the truck that we were glad this was only temporary.

Still, we were excited about being there at last—so excited that even the work of unloading the truck and lugging the bed and dresser upstairs wasn't bad. Loren dollied book cartons down the truck ramp and lined them up three deep along the wall of the oversized garage that we had been assured would give us a lot of storage space. We enjoyed proving to ourselves we could still do physical labor at the advanced age of sixty-two. But oh, were we glad when it was all unloaded and we could go get something to eat! And we were very glad indeed to tuck into bed that night with a view of stars galore through the uncurtained windows. Four days into our retirement, and we were exactly where we wanted to be.

At the same time, I felt the tug of something else, completely at odds with the satisfaction of that moment, an overwhelming sensation not just of having left home, but more than that: of not having a home at all.

PART THREE

On Cerro Espinoso

CHAPTER SEVEN

Building It

ROM CENTRAL Texas to central New Mexico isn't just a lot of miles, it's a lot of difference. From a work life to a retired life is more difference still. Both retiring and moving to a new place to build a house are major life changes—all the more so when they both come at once.

Building a house is taxing. There are so many decisions to make, so many things that can go wrong, so many occasions for worry and anxiety. Yet I look back on the building of our house in New Mexico as a time of excitement and deep satisfaction. Largely, I suppose, because we meant to stay. It tapped very deeply into our nesting instincts.

I had been superficially involved in the building of houses during my first marriage, but never from the initial planning stage, only to the extent of choosing colors and such. Yet, even that I had enjoyed a great deal. In my opinion, leafing through books of wallpaper is one of life's great delights. But building this house was a far greater pleasure, not only because it was to be our *last* house, but also because it was the fulfillment of such a long period of planning and anticipation: a great investment of time and thought and effort. And also, I think, this house was such a pleasure because it was an end in itself. It wasn't a means to the enhancement of lifestyle or an investment for resale; it wasn't a way station or in any sense a moving up. We were building a place where we could just live, just enjoy the days and reflect on it all.

That claim may seem to conflict with our firm intention to continue working after we retired. And indeed we haven't spent much time in reflection, if that means sitting and gazing off into space. But the work we do is, like the house, an end in itself. We do it because we enjoy it; it is simply what we do, who we are. In building our house for retirement, we were trying to construct a place of beauty and comfort that would totally engage the task we were taking up for the rest of our lives: living, being who we are. So far, working is a large part of that. Unlike any of the previous homes we'd shared, this house was to be a home for the whole of life. Before, we'd had our offices and classrooms on campus, and had only secondarily worked at home. Now it was all—working, resting, living—to be in one place.

Since our long meeting with Ray and Joyce and Buddy the previous summer, we had kept closely in touch—sending them the completed spec sheet, asking questions, making minor changes, getting the cost estimate, clarifying points here and there. We felt fully prepared.

We had agreed with Buddy that the launch date would be February 1. We decided on that date after careful consideration. We didn't want him to start too soon and have the walls up before we got there to enjoy the spectacle, but we did want him to get going promptly so we wouldn't have to pay rent any longer than we had to. Foolishly enough, we thought specifying February 1 meant that he would get going on February 1. On the fourth, when we arrived in the East Mountains with our loaded car and rental truck, we pulled off at the Edgewood exit and detoured by our lot before even going to look for our sight-unseen rental in Cedar Crest. We fully expected to see some sign of a beginning—equipment, a pile of rough lumber for concrete forms, something. But there was nothing. We shouldn't have been surprised. For months we had been asking Buddy about a written contract, and none had appeared. Even so, we were disappointed.

We soon learned that it was a good thing he hadn't started before we got there, because if he had we wouldn't have been on hand to determine the exact placement of the house on the lot. And that is a very important decision; once the house is placed, that's that, it's placed. But we hadn't thought about that yet. All we knew when we went by the lot as we drove in was that Buddy hadn't done a thing.

When we finally got him on the phone to ask about it, he seemed awfully casual. "Oh yeah!" he said. "A contract. How about if we meet for coffee day after tomorrow, down at the grill on Highway 14?"

Day after tomorrow—that meant another whole day wasted!

We were going to have many occasions to say that in the months ahead.

A full week after the house was supposed to have been started, we met to fill in the blanks of a generic contract, sign it, and give Buddy our first check to set up a working account. In the space labeled "start date," he filled in "no later than February 15." I had thought he would put, say, the very next day. But we let it go. At least we now had a firm date. Back in the car, we looked at each other and shrugged.

I should explain a little more what it means to build on a cost-plus basis. It was because we were working that way that we needed to set up the working account. Our contract with Buddy specified that we were "owner-builders" and he was being hired as project manager at a fee of 15 percent of total actual costs. Instead of an actual price, we had a detailed estimate. We were to put up certain percentages of the estimate at specified stages in the process, he would deposit our checks in a designated account and write checks on that account to pay for materials and subcontractors, as well as his own draw, and we would settle up at the end.

We would realize over the coming months that this is a risky way to build if you don't keep a good handle on how the costs are running. And as it turned out, we didn't. The regular statements called for in the contract never appeared. We would ask, but it always seemed that the bookkeeper wasn't quite caught up. With most people, this would have made us suspect a scam. With Buddy, it never did. We had full confidence in his integrity from start to finish. What we didn't have full confidence in was his ability to stay on top of things. Some unpleasantness at the end might have been avoided if he had provided reports as he was supposed to or if he had looked ahead and pointed out potential overruns.

Building as an owner-builder does have its advantages, though, if you have the cash. At the very least, it can hold down the cost of interim construction loans, and it keeps you involved in the building of your own house. And certainly we were involved. Except for periods when we were out of town (which turned out to be more than we had expected or wanted), we were there at the site every day. Sometimes we took our camp chairs and sat and watched. It was the best entertainment in town.

February 15 came and went. Nothing happened.

On the morning of the twentieth at nine AM, the phone rang. It was Buddy. Could we meet him at the "site" at nine-thirty? Could we! We went straight to the car and headed for the lot, a half-hour drive away. And that was when we met Angus Campbell.

Angus was our earthmoving contractor. It turned out that he had been studying the plans for some time, as well as studying the slopes and rockiness of the lot, planning the foundation and the septic system. It was Angus who, back in the fall, had dug a test hole that showed this was all going to be harder than we thought; he encountered solid rock that would have to be either drilled or blasted out for both house and septic. (Still very much in evidence, that test hole looked like a grave; I asked him to fill it in and was glad when he did.) On that gray, chilly morning of February 20 we tramped

around the most nearly level part of the lot looking at views, assess-
ing slopes and distances from the property line, considering the
county's limit on height and the approximate footprint of the house,
identifying trees we particularly wanted to save. I began to realize
that this Angus Campbell had a clearer idea of what he was doing
than Buddy did. Not that he marched in and took over; like Buddy,
he was soft-spoken and deferential in manner. But it was clear that
he was the one with the know-how. He was the one who broke out a
laser surveying instrument and talked about wanting to set the house
high enough to maximize our views but not so high as to stick up
conspicuously out of the trees (though it did, after all). Besides, he
had twinkly eyes and an engaging little crooked grin. We liked him.

   I wish we had paused at this point to think about the orientation
of the house on the lot even more carefully than we did. Slopes and
property lines impose their own limitations, of course, but I wish we
had walked around with plans in hand, looking out through what
was going to be the front door or the kitchen window or the patio,
thinking about the angle of light at different times of day. Or better
yet, I wish we had gone out there and done it at different times of
day, to prepare for this moment. If we had, we might not have ended
up with a patio so directly slammed by evening sun that it was
unusable in the summer. But we had thought about it for so long in
relation to the road and the required set-back from the north property line, and had thought so much about the view from the front,
out over the Estancia Basin, that there didn't seem to be anything
else to consider. Any time you're that sure of something, starting to
build a house or anything else, it's probably time to open your mind
and think again. But we didn't. We had been preparing for so long
that we were sure; our minds had closed down. And maybe we could-
n't have done any better anyway.

   So we said yes, here, and Angus sighted some lines with his laser
and put in some markers, and he and his helper made some bright
orange lines on the ground with spray-paint. So where did we want

the driveway to enter? We all trooped down to the road and gazed back up into the lot, walked back and forth, and agreed on a place. He made spray-paint marks for that. Now I thought we were getting somewhere! I expected them to get started right then. But instead they all got back in their pickups, waved to us, and drove off. And nothing else happened for a week.

It might seem as though people temporarily living in a house with great views of the Sandia Mountains would relax, enjoy themselves, and not worry about getting things done. Such people might even go off on rambles to explore other parts of the state. They might drive into the city and see a movie, or visit museums. But no, except for one quick trip to Texas to bring back the other car and our camper trailer, all we did during those initial weeks of waiting for something to happen was stay put and hope for the phone to ring.

At nine AM on February 28, four weeks after the date we had initially designated for the start of construction, the phone finally rang. "I thought you might want to come out to the site," Buddy said. "Angus is here with equipment."

The big day had come at last.

We got there as fast as we could. Angus's helper had broken through from the road with a large earthmover. Scraping out dirt, building dirt up, he smoothed a driveway-width passage across the roadside ditch and through the embankment and worked his way in, up the slope of the lot, pushing down yuccas, chollas, brush. A sign was already up beside the cut with our house number painted in big, crude numerals, and a smaller, neater sign announced the name of Buddy's company. We were official.

This was all to the good. Yet I couldn't help feeling how irremediably altered—wounded—our patch of earth was now. I was eager to see this house built, but at the same time I regretted that our land on the ridge was no longer the way it had been when we first saw it.

It was a cold day, with dry pellets of snow in the air. Hugging ourselves in our jackets, we hung around until noon. Loren took pic-

February 28, 2002.
Breaking through the roadside embankment for the driveway.

tures. We grinned at each other. Buddy walked this way and that, watching more than supervising. Clearly, Angus didn't need supervision.

It was he who came over from time to time to ask us questions— mainly, how badly did we want to save this or that tree. In particular, there was the question of a good-sized piñon sitting squarely in the middle of the most direct path for the driveway. He figured we would want to keep that one, right? You bet we did! So which side of it did we want the driveway to go? Hmm, between the tree and the corner of the house, we guessed. OK, he said, then he'd better push up a couple of big rocks to keep the subs and delivery trucks from running into it.

"Oh," he added, "I'll do the same all around the perimeter of the work site, bulldoze rocks up, try to limit how far they pull their trucks in and stack material. Try to minimize the damage to the lot. Then at the end spread out the rocks."

We nodded. We could see what a good idea it was.

"Or actually, most of 'em will go on the low side of the slope anyway, to shore up the pad and foundation."

"Yes," we said, "of course"—as if we had known it all along.

When the house was all finished and the workmen gone, our nice piñon sat there in an oval of earth, surrounded by the white gravel of the driveway, guarded by two big rocks. My study window overlooked it, and I kept watch over it, and sometimes carried it buckets of water.

All through that first exciting but sad day, trees came down and rocks were gouged out. We had realized by then that Angus was a man who cared about trees, but even so, he and his crew committed a painful devastation on our land as they cleared the footprint of the house and the septic field and the working area. They violated it and made it ugly.

I had known full well that trees have to come down and land has to be scraped and leveled if you're going to build a house. You have to break eggs to make an omelet. But I learned that where these particular two-and-a-half acres were concerned, I couldn't be detached about it. In the years since we had bought our land we'd tramped around and imagined where the house would go, and more than once we'd shifted our ideas because this or that tree—even this or that cactus—would be wiped out. Now we couldn't even remember which ones we had wanted to save; it all looked so different, so many were crunched over and piled up as waste. Until this stage of the building process was finished, I had mixed feelings about being there to watch.

From groundbreaking to the pouring of stem walls for the foundation took a full month because the ground was so rocky that the necessary preparatory work was more extensive than anyone had imagined. Angus brought in heavy equipment and then heavier equipment, and they pounded and broke rock and pounded and broke it some more. He had to dynamite for the septic system. Then there was a slight delay before the pouring of the slab when Loren discovered, only the evening before the concrete trucks were scheduled to arrive, that the rough-out plumbing had placed a toilet smack in the middle of what was to be a bedroom.

Pulverizing rock, preparing the foundation.

At that point we realized that we couldn't count on Buddy to check for errors.

During this slow period of preparation, he had us start making choices. We had thought that with all our advance planning, this would all be easy. It wasn't. We still had to go through all the usual steps in the usual order. And there were a lot of them—which meant lots of steps to trip over.

The first was kitchen cabinets. Another of Buddy's nine o'clock phone calls, just out of the blue, sent us hurrying off to meet him at a wholesaler's. We had to do this now, he said, to make sure the cabinets were made up and on hand when it was time to put them in.

To me, kitchen cabinets are one of the most important parts of a house. I cook a lot—not elaborately, but more or less every day—and my kitchen needs to have plenty of storage and counter space. It needs to be pleasant to work in. So we had already done a good bit of looking at cabinets in home supply stores. We had picked up catalogs of two or three brands, and Loren had worked out an actual plan—so many 24" base cabinets, so many 30", a corner turn-around, and so forth. We were also quite clear on the wood and finish—we wanted natural-finish maple. But here I think our advance preparation actually did us a disservice. We were so sure we knew what we wanted that we didn't treat this big choice with the care it deserved. We went to the wholesaler's thinking there wasn't going to be much to talk about.

Wrong! For one thing, it turned out that even though we had specified maple on the spec sheet, the estimate Buddy had given us was based on oak. When his initial estimate had come in higher than we expected, we had asked how we might trim it down and he had decided on his own that oak cabinets would be fine. On that basis, Sam the cabinet man (not his real name either) had put down something like seven thousand dollars as the final estimate. Considering the number of cabinets our plans called for, and not just in the kitchen, that didn't sound bad. So when we met that day, we were feeling fine until we found out what they had done. No, we said, we wanted what we'd said we wanted: maple.

The two of them exchanged glances. "Uh," Sam said, "that'll run a little more." At least, that's how I remembered it. Much later, when this became a point of dispute, Buddy remembered that he had said it would be a couple of thousand more. But it didn't really matter which of us was remembering right, because neither was even close. The final bill was more than double the original estimate—quite a shock at the end, when it was too late to do anything about it.

I've kept asking myself why we didn't say "thank you very much but we're going to do some comparison shopping." It simply didn't occur to us. We assumed that our man Buddy knew where to get the best product for the best price, and we didn't even raise the question of looking elsewhere. We did notice that the drawers Sam was showing us were not mitered, as the ones we had looked at earlier had been, but we let it pass. We didn't think to ask which parts of these cabinets were going to be made of solid wood and which of plywood and whether any parts were going to be particle board. Big mistake.

Choosing doors was a snap by comparison, though again, I wonder why we didn't shop around and compare prices. And as to hardware, when we reminded Buddy and Sam that we had specified brushed nickel hinges and handles—not knobs but levered handles, to make life easier on arthritic wrists—they exchanged another uneasy glance. I don't know whether we were bumping up against a lowball estimate again or this place didn't have brushed nickel. In any event, Sam suggested we consider brushed stainless. He went back to his warehouse and returned with a knob and hinge. OK, we said; that'll be fine. But it wasn't. After everything was installed, the brushed stainless had a harsh look very different from the warm friendliness (so we had come to think, attaching significance to everything that went into this house) of brushed nickel. We knew what we wanted, so why didn't we stick with it?

One reason was that careful comparison shopping on all these many choices would have meant a big investment of time. Of course, we could have taken all the time in the world; we were retired. But we were retired professors. We needed to prove (to ourselves; no one else was watching) that, paycheck or no paycheck, we were going to keep up our work—that is, keep writing papers and articles and books. We couldn't squander time on mere shopping. In an absolute sense, of course, carrying on our work was the important thing. Ideas are always more important than objects. But at that moment, the important thing was building our house. We should have stayed focused on that.

Fortunately, we did learn enough from the cabinet and door experience to assert ourselves when it came to choosing other things, like appliances and floor tile and carpet and paint. We went where Buddy sent us, but we also went elsewhere and spent time comparing selection and cost. And sometimes we told him, "No, get it at this other place."

There was something else, though, besides our obsession with keeping up our work, that constrained our time for doing the careful looking and considering that was needed. During those same early weeks of the construction process we were run ragged with other problems and decisions, first selling our house in Texas and then something far more serious.

We had listed our house on the market the first of January, knowing it was a slow time of year for real estate but nevertheless expecting that we might get some quick action on such a nice house. When we drove away on February 2 we had had precisely one looker. By early March we had begun to get seriously discouraged. But then we received not one but two offers, on the same day. The two were very close on price but differed on various details, and we debated which to accept. We seesawed between them, trying to balance the pluses and minuses. Then once we decided (on a young couple buying their first house) we were still uncertain for a couple of weeks whether the deal was going to go through. There was some kind of insurance crisis back in Texas, and purchasers were having trouble getting coverage. But one thing we did know for sure, we were going to need the money very soon.

All this was nothing, compared to the real blow: the sudden collapse of our arrangements for Doug, which we had thought were so secure. The sale of the house had gone through, and we were back in Bryan to sign the papers and move out—doing it ourselves again but with a really big rental truck this time. I was in fact about fifteen minutes away from speaking at the opening of a library exhibit on the history of women at Texas A&M, actually going over in my mind what I was going to say, when my cell phone rang and I got the news that Doug's residential facility was closing.

I was stunned. We had been through this once before, when the San Angelo home closed. At least this time it came with some advance notice; we had two months to find him another place. That is not an easy thing to do for a blind and mentally disabled adult. And there wasn't a thing we could do about it right then, because we had to finish loading the truck with everything we owned except what little we had already taken with us, and drive back to New

Mexico. The rental house was now going to serve as a warehouse as well as an interim place to live.

The very next day after we got back to Cedar Crest and got unloaded, I started making phone calls. First I called the social worker, Wayne, who had done so much for Doug over the years. He was working hard at that end to find placements for not just one, but twenty—all of them, including Doug, anxious and fearful. In a couple of weeks Wayne put together a list of possibilities and helped me narrow it down to two, so when Loren and I drove back to Fort Worth to help Doug decide, we could take him to visit just those two, and not get confused. And between the two, the choice was easy. The first was a high-rise; he could never have navigated those elevators and multiple turns, and if he'd accidentally gone out one of the unguarded exits he could have been lost on the sidewalk. The second place was also larger and more complicated in layout than where he had been living, but at least it was all on one floor. And it was much cleaner and better maintained than the old place, which toward the end had actually smelled. Moreover, several of the people Doug knew had already decided to move there, and he wanted to be with them. In a flurry of activity, we got everything settled in one day and hit the now familiar road back to New Mexico with the date set for us to come back and move him in a month.

In April, with the slab poured at last, we set off on a long-scheduled trip to Italy, where Loren had a conference to attend. We were reluctant to leave. We wondered how many things might go wrong and not be caught. And indeed the framers did measure wrong or read the plans wrong, something, with the result that our entry hall lost its carefully worked out symmetry.

By this time, Buddy, a man who'd never been farther from New Mexico than Colorado, was convinced that we must be the world's biggest travelers. We were never able to convince him that it wasn't usually like this. Before we retired we had rarely been able to go along to each other's conferences or speaking trips, and we had long looked forward to the time when we could do so. This was the first such opportunity—a meeting on the shores of Lake Como. We had bought our tickets weeks before we knew about having to move Doug or having to do our own construction foreman work.

The famous lake proved to be as beautiful as its reputation indicates—at least, on days when we could see it through the fog and mist. The weather was not at all what one expects of sunny Italy. Fortunately, compulsive as ever, I had taken along the manuscript of a book I had in progress and spent much of my time, those cold and rainy days, working in our hotel room. We did have a nice excursion up to Bellagio and a wet one by train to the little town of Lugano, in Switzerland, and at the end the weather cleared up pretty well for the day we had planned in Milan. As we started to the airport for our flight back to Albuquerque, the clouds finally lifted all the way and we saw, for the first time, the beautiful peaks of the Alps. We honestly had not known they were so close. It was wonderful looking down on them from the plane as we took off.

We had gone away happy in the knowledge that we had a foundation. When we returned and drove up our dirt road on the ridge, we saw for the first time the vertical evidence that we were going to have a house there. The framers had most of the studs up for the walls and were already starting on the roof trusses. It was an exciting moment. We stopped for Loren to take a picture before going on up to take a closer look.

Of all the various subcontractors who came and went, the framers were the team we most enjoyed watching. How I wished we hadn't missed a minute of what they did! Of course, I wouldn't have wanted to miss Italy either. Working in twos or threes, always so well-coordinated and well balanced and bold as they walked along those narrow boards high above the concrete carrying heavy trusses, they

April 19, 2002. Mostly framed and partially roof-decked.

May 4, 2002, my sixty-third birthday. Through another door.

were truly a spectacle. This was the only phase of construction when Buddy wouldn't let us go up close to watch. They were using nail guns, he pointed out, and if one went astray it could take out an eye. And there was also the risk of things falling on us if we walked underneath them. But we could watch from a distance, and after they finished for the day we could walk through the maze of two-by-fours and imagine rooms.

Now progress was fast. It was actually becoming a house. By the first of May it was weathered in, with sheathing and roof deck on, windows and outside doors in. Even the expensive red-tinted concrete of the patio and the front steps and porch was in place and looking good.

On my birthday, May 4, the same exciting day when we first saw the framing of the fireplace and hearth, we met another of the most memorable characters of this whole experience: Charlie, the electrician. When we drove up the driveway—not graveled yet but passable if you didn't worry about nails—we saw a pickup with a covered bed parked on the concrete apron outside the garage, and then, as we walked up, a camp chair, table, and grill set up inside the garage. We heard a radio somewhere. And when we walked into the house, between the studs, we encountered this bearded bear of a man, with one bad eye and a no-nonsense manner.

He had driven up from Mountainair, he said, where he lived with his mother, and would be more or less camping out on site while he did the wiring. We knew immediately that we were going to enjoy this guy, but also realized pretty quickly that if we wanted him to get any work done, we'd better not get him started talking. Loren would come to have less patience with Charlie's gabbing and his do-it-his-own-way approach than I did, but we count him among our outstanding memories. We invited him to our celebration dinner at the end.

Once Charlie had finished, the metal roof went on, beautifully reflecting the sky in its shiny silver. Then the Sheetrock went up, and we could clearly see the dimensions of rooms. We began to ask

Buddy when we could expect to move in. End of May, he said. Middle of June at the latest.

We would learn not to take such projections seriously.

Around the middle of May we drove to Fort Worth again to move Doug to his new residence. He had lived at the old one for fifteen years, and it was a very difficult transition for him. He had a terrible time learning his way around. One day when his psychologist was working with him on learning the routes between places he was most often to go, he took a wrong turn and demanded to be taken back to his room. There he fell on his knees beside his bed, beating his fists on the mattress and crying. If I had been living nearby during those weeks, my forty-three-year-old son might never have regained even the limited degree of independence he'd had before. As it was, as I monitored all this from six hundred miles away, the feelings of guilt that are always lurking in the shadows for a parent of a handicapped child started coming out of hiding, with consequences we didn't face for months to come.

But if Doug's move was hard on him, we soon realized that it was a blessing in disguise. Not only had the old place smelled so stale and been so obviously ill-kept, we began to realize that with absolutely no choice of menu he hadn't been eating well there, to the point that his health had suffered. He pronounced the food at his new place "ten times better!" and began to gain a little weight.

The day the interior painting was completed was another big occasion.

Paint had probably been the hardest of our choices. We knew we wanted our same muted dark green for the bedroom, a light but not white for everywhere else, and of course white ceilings, with white

wood trim both inside and out, and a red front door. The red for the
door was easy; there weren't many choices. The green was almost as
easy. We quickly settled on a shade the color chart called "Critter's
Drum," though I'm sure whoever named it must have meant
"Critter's Dream." It was dark, cool, and soothing but at the same
time rather dramatic—a color that a critter might well dream of. But
finding what we had for the light-not-white walls everywhere else
wasn't so easy. I had pictured a sort of whispery taupe with a hint of
the lavender overtone that the desert takes on when you look out
over a long vista. Yet although there were more off-white chips than
anyone could imagine, not one of them seemed to capture that quality. We spent hours at the paint store and hours more gazing at chips
taped up on the walls of the rental house, using their brown as a base
for comparison. Loren got thoroughly tired of it and even the tiniest
bit cross. Finally we settled on a pale taupe that we hoped we would
like.

The day I first saw it on the wall, it took my breath away, it was
so perfect. And it changed in different lights, from sometimes merely
gray to lavender to sometimes rose. I loved it.

The last choice we made was the stucco for the outside walls.
Buddy gave us a color chart to carry around and look at, and for a
while we kept stopping whenever we saw a building that looked good
to us, to hold our color chips against it and compare. In the end,
what we picked turned out to be pinker than we expected, and we
regretted not choosing something closer to the color of the earth.
Standing inside and looking out, the exterior color and the beautiful
interior wall color didn't complement each other. We also regretted
that we hadn't chosen the bright green roof instead of "traditional"
silver. Green would have cost more, and we were being prudent, but
after it was done I wished we had gone with our inclination. How
many roofs were we going to choose, after all? On the other hand, it
was fine as it was. So was the stucco. These things weren't really life
altering decisions. They only seemed like it at the time.

Then, at almost the very end, Charlie came back and we discovered a mistake on my part that cost him a full extra day's work. And electricians don't come cheap.

Early on, maybe even the day we first met him, Charlie had asked whether I wanted white switch plates or ivory ones. Hmm, ivory, white, ivory, white—maybe white would be a bit stark? "Ivory," I said, and thought no more about it. He finished the wiring and went away until it was time to come back and do the finish work.

In late June—three weeks after Buddy had guessed we would be moving in—Charlie and a helper came back to hang light fixtures, attach plug sockets, and put up switch plates. Usually, with things moving so fast, we dropped by the house once in the morning and again in the afternoon. Unfortunately, that day we didn't get by until nearly quitting time. They were nearly finished. The painters were there too, doing touch-up, and when one of them gestured toward a switch plate and frowned, I saw at once that the ivory wouldn't do. It was ugly against the paint color. They would have to be changed out for white, that was all there was to it. Which meant the sockets would also have to be changed.

Charlie had already told us he was behind schedule for getting to another job, and he was not a bit happy about it when I told him. He actually roared at me, "I asked you!" True, but that was then, and now it was plain to see that I had chosen wrong. The atmosphere in the house became stormy. We cut our look-see short and slipped out to our car.

We were just about to pull away when Charlie came hustling up. "My helper said I was a little rude in there," he said. "Don't worry, I'll change 'em out. It'll mean another day's work." Another day's worth of labor charges, he meant, besides the cost of the materials.

"Of course," we said. "It's not your fault, after all."

I apologized. "I should have stopped to think. But you can see for yourself that the ivory just won't do with our paint, right?"

He shrugged. "I don't concern myself with colors."

❖

Buddy's estimate of our move-in date had long since been pushed back from early June to mid-June to the end of the month. Now even that began to look doubtful. Not until June 21 did Angus resume work on the septic field, and the house couldn't be occupied until that, for one, had all passed inspection.

Then there was the matter of the porch railing called for on the plans. Oh yeah, Buddy said. What kind did we want? You know, we said, a porch railing. Nothing fancy. If you're going to sit in rocking chairs on the front porch, you want a porch railing. Besides, there was that rocky slope not six feet from the end of the porch; we couldn't have grandchildren running off the end of the porch and falling down that. So he got the trim carpenter back out, and after five minutes of doodling on the back of an envelope the carpenter had us a porch railing designed. But that meant, of course, a couple of more days' work.

Even worse, the cabinets we'd ordered with such a sense of urgency back in March still hadn't shown up. Sam the cabinet man

The (almost) finished product.

had come and measured after the Sheetrock was in, but that was the last we'd heard. Then suddenly, only a few days before the end of the month, there they were, all in boxes, filling the garage. It was startling how many. There was no way all those cabinets could be installed by the thirtieth, not to mention the other odds and ends that needed doing, and we had already given notice on our rental.

Incredibly, the cabinet installation took only a single day, June 28. But one day was enough to show us what a disaster Sam truly was. In the kitchen, they didn't fit right but could be made to work with a little shimming and shifting. In the master bath they didn't even come close. The two tall bookcases for beside the entry hadn't been ordered at all. And the living room built-ins had arrived with no tops! You looked down into holes where the shelves would be. Two days until our supposed move-in, and the cabinets were a mess. There were no kitchen countertops, and therefore the sink had not been installed; the counters and shower liners in the bathroom hadn't even been ordered because the marble people had to wait to measure the cabinets, which now didn't fit; appliances were sitting in boxes; and the electrical inspector who was supposed to have come two days ago hadn't shown up. But then, it was just as well he hadn't, because the things he was supposed to inspect weren't all done yet.

Just a few more days, Buddy said. Fourth of July weekend for sure.

That was cutting it close. I had to be at Texas A&M on the tenth for the oral exam of my last Ph.D. student. But what could we do? We reserved a rental truck (doing it ourselves again, of course) for the fifth through seventh. That meant three working days to go until we were supposed to pick up the truck and move.

On Monday, July 1, the kitchen counters, sink, dishwasher, range, and oven were all installed. (We discovered some time later that the oven was just sitting there in the cabinet loose, definitely a safety issue, but oh well.) Someone had figured out that the missing cabinets in the bathroom could be slipped into place later, so the counter people went ahead and took measurements. But the electrical inspector still hadn't shown up, and it was a short week because of the holiday.

By the afternoon of the third, still no inspector. We couldn't move in until he had passed the work.

The fourth came and went without a word from Buddy. What to do? On the morning of the fifth, Friday, we crossed our fingers, picked up the truck, and started loading. About mid-morning he dropped by the rental house while Loren was tying a piece of furniture on. He stood looking sadly at what we were doing. "The inspector got there late Wednesday," he said. "Bad news. We didn't pass."

Charlie, it seemed, had failed to install a smoke detector in a place required by the building code. True, we had more smoke detectors total than we were required to have, but we didn't have one *there.*

We looked at the truck. We looked at Buddy.

"The inspector said you could go ahead and bring stuff into the garage," he said. "Just be sure to keep it out in the middle, away from the walls. He has to be able to see every outlet again."

We looked at the truck again and sighed. This meant moving in and yet not moving in. At least we could haul things over before we had to start for Texas. But how were we going to be able to get all our furniture and all the boxes, everything we owned, into one single pile in the middle of the garage?

"You can put some of it inside," he mumbled, "just keep it away from the walls."

By the time we were done on Saturday afternoon we had more or less a mountain in the garage and little hills in the middle of rooms. David and Angi had come and helped—a good thing, since Loren's arthritis had flared up and one knee was trying to give out from under him. We couldn't possibly have done it without them, even with hired help for the piano. After two big loads of heavy things, we assured them we could finish out the small stuff ourselves, and they left, but that last load just about killed us. I fell into a state of sullen rebellion when Loren insisted that we were honor-bound to go back and do a thorough cleanup job at the rental house, not just make a gesture at it. He was right, of course. He usually is. But oh how thankful I was when we finally finished and turned that truck back in! The happiest thing I could think of, at that moment, was that I would be able to end my life without ever renting a moving truck again.

Doing our own moving for the third time in six months taught us something about aging—it comes in jumps, rather than a steady incline. In only the few months since we had left Bryan with a few odds and ends our physical strength had waned dramatically.

I should add that when the house was "finished" and ready to move into, it wasn't in fact finished. For four more months workmen were in and out finishing up odds and ends that should have been done long before—a hole in the ceiling where someone had fallen through, a phone line not connected, the missing counter tops, a leaking shower head. We finally got tired of it and called a halt, and Loren did the last few things himself, or else we gave up and left them undone. We had learned that there is no such thing as getting everything perfect. You just can't. There are too many details, too many places for workers to make mistakes, too many things you may fail to notice.

But we also learned that in the long run it doesn't matter. We were happy in our new home and loved it even if it wasn't perfect. That's how it is in life, isn't it? Our children aren't perfect, but we love them anyway. We know we aren't perfect ourselves, but we love each other in spite of our mess-ups. Schools and churches may not be perfect, but they still add meaning to our lives. And so it is with houses.

We turned in the truck the afternoon of July seventh and left for Texas early on the morning of the eighth. We stopped in Fort Worth that night to check on Doug, then drove on to College Station on the ninth. On the tenth my student defended his dissertation, and we immediately set out for League City, on past Houston nearly to Galveston. We couldn't quite make it in time for our granddaughter Melissa's birthday, but the next morning, we took her out to breakfast. By nightfall on the eleventh we were halfway back to New Mexico. We were becoming proficient at fast car trips.

Only when we stopped at the motel that night did Loren admit that he was having major trouble with his right leg, the leg that had started hurting during the move. When I saw how swollen it was, I wanted to look for medical help right then, but he refused, insisting that we get home first.

The next day we drove tensely on, not knowing what was wrong. When we finally pulled into our driveway about four in the afternoon, we were exhausted. How wonderful it would have been if the big mountain and several hills of stuff had somehow moved and assembled themselves while we were gone, like the skeletons coming together in the Valley of Dry Bones! But no such luck; there it all was, just as we had left it. And even then Loren refused to phone his doctor until we had put our bed together and put sheets on it, just as we had when we dragged in dog-tired at the sight-unseen house five months earlier. Only when the bed was ready to fall into did he call his rheumatologist. I had taken measurements of the two legs for comparison, and when she heard the numbers she told him to go straight to the emergency room, it might be a blood clot. Deep blood clots in the leg are serious business.

An emergency room is the last place you want to be on a Friday night in any city in America. The system being what it is, emergency rooms are where the poor go to get primary medical care, not to mention the fact that they're crowded due to the uptick in accidents and violence on Friday and Saturday nights. As a result, they're awful places to be stuck in—crowded, noisy, and miserably slow. We were there from 5:15 until long after midnight.

David, who is himself a nurse, came down, and he and Angi waited with us for part of that time. He checked the leg himself and told us what to expect, then shared our relief when the Doppler exam showed there wasn't a blood clot. The trouble was a burst Baker's cyst behind the knee. No wonder it had caused so much pain—which, in his typical fashion, Loren hadn't said so much as a word about until the ordeal was nearly over.

At three in the morning we again pulled into the driveway of our new home and parked on the apron of the garage. When we stepped out of the car and closed the doors, we were left in the deep darkness of our mountain ridge thirty miles from the city. We looked up into the night sky to the most dazzling array of stars spread out against the deepest, clearest black either of us had ever seen. A miracle of stars. We clutched each other and grinned, craning our necks to take in the wonder of it. If Loren's leg hadn't been so badly out of commission we might actually have danced. Yes! This was what we had moved here for!

CHAPTER EIGHT

Being There

O UR HOUSE ON THE RIDGE was a fine place to learn to
be retired. Once we got settled, our days fell into a comfortable rhythm. I wrote and quilted and read. Loren
wrote and built a shed and read. We met at lunch and talked and
then went back to what we were doing. The hours seemed as spacious as the high desert country around us. There was always that
semi-arid spectacle just outside the window, and I could walk out
into it whenever I felt like it. If I sat on the porch to read, it was right
there when I looked up from my page. It all amounted to this: I
became quieter in mind. I planted sweet clover on the septic field
and carried water to it every day in buckets. For the first time in my
life I started keeping a journal. This chapter will incorporate, here
and there, bits and pieces of that sporadic record I kept of our days.

SETTLING IN

Through the rest of July, after we moved in, and most of August we
had hot weather—a convection-oven kind of heat utterly unlike
that of Texas. The monsoon season never really arrived that year.
Some days, by late afternoon, we found ourselves wondering if it had
been a good idea to build without air conditioning, relying solely on
windows and ceiling fans. Yet after years of living closed-up against
heat and humidity I was glad to have the windows open. And the
nights could be counted on to cool off. We rarely even turned on the
ceiling fan above our bed.

Many nights we did indeed hear coyotes. Before we retired, while we were waiting and planning for our house, we had listened to the computer encyclopedia's rendition of coyotes—and also to wolves, though we knew we wouldn't have any of those—but that hadn't prepared us for the pleasure of the real thing. There are plenty of coyotes in Texas, of course. Jeanie's husband says they only have to go outdoors any night of the week, there in Weatherford, to hear them. But for me that's a New Mexico experience. Sometimes when I got up in the night to go to the bathroom I would hear them yammering. I would stand at the window and listen and feel the breeze, and if I had my glasses on I could look out at a blanket of stars.

We had such great skies! With our thin, dry air and freedom from light pollution, because the main ridge of the Sandias was between us and Albuquerque, nights were a deep, clear black that showed up the swoosh of the Milky Way and even the faint Pleiades. Days, a magical clear blue that varied from pale to intense, nothing but blue, sometimes with an isolated white puff or two. When storms came up, the roiling thunderheads were splendid.

Tony Hillerman, the Four Corners mystery writer, commented once that reviewers of his novels sometimes complained of how he was always interrupting the forward motion of the plot with descriptions of clouds. But why not? He lived in New Mexico, after all, and he kept his eyes open.

I remember an evening when we had some people over and were just sitting down to dinner. I had taken my chair when I happened to glance at the view out the window and broke into the conversation. "Look!" I pointed out at the sky. The full moon was just swimming up out of the Estancia Basin with an astonishing peachy glow. Other times I glanced up from a page to see bolts of lightning playing over those same plains, eastward toward Moriarty.

The sky somehow became more a part of our lives.

Toward the end of August that first summer we arranged for Doug to fly out for his birthday. We wanted him to get a sense of the

Rainbow in the big sky out over the Estancia Basin.

new house right away, so he could think about us in a context and start attaching a sense of home to it himself. The second evening he was there, I was doing something or other at the computer after dinner and became aware that he was standing at my shoulder. I recorded the moment in my journal that night:

> *Suddenly he was just there. He had made his way in from the living room, no problem. Either he hadn't made a sound or I was too involved in revising my chapter to notice. The window was open, of course, and just then, very distinctly, a coyote howled— not a whole chorus of them, this time, and not with any preliminary yipping, just a single howl.*
>
> *I asked him, "Did you hear that?"*
>
> *"Yeah," he breathed.*
>
> *"It was a coyote."*
>
> *He said it again, the same way, with a tone of wonder, "Yeah."*
>
> *And the thing is, something about the way he said it convinced me that he really did know it was a coyote, without being told. I don't know how he could have, unless maybe he'd heard*

the coyote howls on our computer in Bryan. Anyway, he seemed to recognize it for what it was. I don't know, I just really liked that.

We had resolved to do more walking after we retired, and Loren quickly established a habit of walking down the hill every morning before breakfast to get our newspaper. I am never as disciplined about such things as he is, but even I went walking nearly every day. Sometimes that meant only an easy ramble around our own land. Except for its dustiness, our road was a good place for walking. For the energetic, the road made a complete loop. Or on days when I felt really ambitious I walked with Loren down to pick up our mail, only a mile-and-a-half round trip but steep on the return. Woe to him or her who forgot a hat! The desert-country sun beats down hard. But as fall came—earlier than we were used to in Texas—and the heat eased off, we walked more.

Any time I went rambling on the uneven terrain of our two-and-a-half acres, I kept a sharp watch for the moist black pellets that meant deer were still coming around, in spite of our having moved in. I also watched for little piñon inchlings. Often they were to be found poking up within a clump of cactus or yucca, which, like the junipers, provided a patch of shade or shelter from the wind to help the less hardy get going.

Before, when we had still been waiting to retire, only visiting these acres once or twice a year and thinking how it was going to be to build our house, I had imagined grubbing out most of the cactus and leaving just a few choice specimens. Now we knew that wouldn't be a good idea, even if it was feasible. Plant life there on the ridge all hung together. And besides its sheltering of piñon seedlings, cactus was important in holding the soil when we got one of our rare hard rains. Still, it was undeniably a disadvantage for walking around. We realized just how much of a disadvantage when Doug made his first visit. We naturally wanted to take him outdoors, and he wanted to go, but at nearly every step he was at risk of planting his foot in a clump of spines. With anyone else, we could have said "watch out for the cactus." But that wouldn't have helped him a bit; he wouldn't know which way to flinch. We had to keep jerking him by the arm, which was tiresome for all of us. So when the weather turned cool, I started clearing a cactus-free strip from the house to the garden spot. At least we would have that much of a navigable path for when he came again.

It was slow going. I didn't even try to tackle the big chollas, of course, but even limiting myself to the prickly pears and the claret cups, there were just so many of them, and with such very long roots. And then there was the problem of what to do with them. If you just dig up a cactus and leave it, it puts down new roots and all you've done is propagate it. All I could figure out was to pile it on more out-of-the-way cacti or yuccas that would hold them up away from the ground. Certainly we couldn't pile them up and burn them. We might set the whole ridge on fire. I persevered until I had a path by which we could walk Doug up to the garden if we went very carefully, but for the most part our *cerro* remained *espinoso*.

There was another way, too, in which Prickly Ridge lived up to its name: porcupines.

We had seen, back in the spring when the house was just under way, that something was stripping the bark off piñon trees, leaving yellow wounds on the trunks and curled-up strips of bark on the ground. At first we supposed deer were doing it, but Angus, a true outdoorsman, said no, it was porcupines. Until then I don't suppose I'd ever seen a porcupine outside a zoo. But as summer went on we sometimes saw them along the roads, not always dead, and after we moved in Loren started seeing them when he made his early morning walk for the newspaper. The stripping of bark continued, and we were worried about losing our piñons. So we drove up to the county seat, Santa Fe, and checked out a trap from the animal control office—not a foot-mangling trap, of course; a drop-door one. When we asked the officer what to use for bait, he didn't have a clue, but after making a couple of phone calls he came up with two suggestions: piñon bark or fruit.

Why, we wondered, would a porcupine go into a cage to get bark when there was piñon bark all around, free for the stripping? So we tried pieces of apple, orange, dried apricots. Loren set the trap first in one place and then in another. The bait was stolen several times, and once we caught a rabbit that grazed placidly beside our feet when we released it, but no porcupine. About that same time, though, we started noticing a strong odor when we passed a certain culvert a little way up the road and when we checked it out we found an abundance of droppings near the end on the high side. When Loren scrambled down the drop-off to where he could look through from the low side, he saw at least one porcupine curled up inside. So he set the trap near the high end where they had been coming out and pooping, and this time, at Charlie the electrician's suggestion, baited it with salt nuggets. We had our porcupine the second morning.

Our idea was to transport it over to Sandia Peak, to the national forest. But the problem then became how to move the cage. Porky flared his quills every time we got close, and they reached past the handle. Loren didn't trust his work gloves to protect him if he just picked it up. But true to his calling (the word engineer comes from the French for ingenuity) he found that a two-by-four would slide neatly through the handle, and one on each end, we were able to carry the cage between us to our garage. Loading it into the back of our mini-SUV was a bit awkward, but we managed, first spreading some newspapers in case of a social lapse.

Our porcupine turned out to be quite a charming animal. With his quills at rest he looked pretty much like a dead bush, but when he flared them they showed a nice variegated golden color underneath. And he had such bright little black button eyes. I

liked the little guy, and while we drove the twenty or so miles
toward the peak I pretended to talk to him (primarily to amuse
Loren, of course). "Now, Porky, it's going to be colder up here.
You're going to have to find a good place to curl up in the winter
time."

We used the two-by-four again to unload him and set the
cage down at the edge of the road, and Loren lifted the door. Out
came Porky at once, and waddled and scuttled his way down the
hill. He was going over a log the last time we saw him.

Fall came early at that high elevation. The days turned sunny
and cool, with cold nights. When we heard there was to be a meteor
shower, we figured we were in a perfect place to watch it, so on the
night it was supposed to be at its peak we set up our camp chairs on
the apron of the garage, put on our jackets, and went out to watch.

The paper had said the meteors would appear to emanate
from the general direction of the Pleiades. Sometimes I can see
that little bundle of stars and sometimes not, but once we found
them we knew the area to watch. We leaned way back in our
chairs, to look up without getting a crick in the neck, and waited.
After a while I went in and brought out a couple of lap robes to
wrap up in. We never saw any meteors, but lots of stars. It was
great.

That first Thanksgiving was nice, but strange. We had been used
to having at least a fair-sized group, always including Doug. This year,
though, he went to his father's instead, and only David and Angi
came to eat turkey with us. They were always good company, but
with just four of us at the table it seemed like a greatly attenuated
feast. When they left about dark to drive back through Tijeras

Canyon into the city, we told them to drive carefully and stood on the front porch waving them out the driveway. I thought I discerned a pattern setting in.

Soon after that, on December third, we got our first snow.

It started in the morning and picked up steadily all day. As it happened, I had planned a dinner party that evening to celebrate Loren's birthday. By then we had met a group of people who were fast becoming friends. And it had indeed come about by way of church, though not the way we expected. We had promised ourselves, before we moved, that if we became churchgoers again, it wouldn't be at a church down in the city, but out in the East Mountains where we were going to be living. And as soon as we arrived and moved into the sight-unseen rental, we began visiting churches, but nothing clicked. Then I read about a Presbyterian church in the city whose pastor was active in a community advocacy group that the mayor had called "a bunch of left-wing radicals." Interesting! I thought. So I waited until Loren was out of town for a conference and, with a sensation of sneaky betrayal, drove into the city on Sunday morning and was hooked. Once Loren agreed to give it a try, La Mesa Presbyterian and its people became the solid rock of our life.

Most of the guests at his birthday party, then, were driving out from Albuquerque, and it wasn't snowing down there, only raining, so I phoned them all and offered to put the party off to the next night. Nah, they said, they weren't scared of a little snow. Sure enough, it turned out not to be a good night for driving in the East Mountains. We got about eight inches. When Loren drove over to rugged Tijeras to pick up Fred, who couldn't drive at night, he nearly slid into a car parked at the bottom of the steep driveway and did back over three solar lights buried under the snow. Then Stu, the retired theology professor who had insisted he wasn't afraid of a little snow, got his car stuck in our driveway and had to be shoveled out. It all seemed rather hilarious, and our hardship party took its place in the group lore.

After wondering whether we would get acquainted in the new place, here we were, only a few months later, with a circle of new friends willing to drive thirty miles out from town in a snowstorm for a birthday dinner. And only a few days later, with snow still hushing our quiet ridge into silence, our longtime friends Beth and Roy took the trouble of flying out from Maryland to see our new place. We tramped over the lot together, slipped down on slopes, and sat on bancos at a little country café to eat fiery-hot New Mexico dishes. Then they went home, and we returned to the quiet rhythm of our days.

A week later, Alan and Shanna flew out for a weekend. I wished the children had come, but we had a good time with just the two of them.

We went to Santa Fe today for the usual walking around, stopped at the Hendersons' in Golden to buy a few Christmas presents, and all came back pretty tired. Shanna went to bed early, but there was to be another meteor shower and Alan wanted to see it, so the two of us stayed up late. About midnight we went out on the front steps to watch. It was cold enough that

Snowy view from our front door.

*we didn't stay long, but we must have seen half a dozen bright
streaks across the sky. I'll remember it—I mean, not only seeing
the meteors, but seeing them with this son of mine who hasn't
been around much these past few years.*

A week before Christmas it snowed again—on the very day
Loren had intended to drive into the city to do his shopping. I tried
to persuade him not to go, because of the roads; insisted that I
wouldn't care if I didn't have a present; but he went anyway and
made it there and back safely. Then Doug flew out to spend a
week—not as easy a trip to organize as I had expected. He had lost
the services of his social worker. This meant I had to enlist his
father's assistance for getting him to the airport, and apparently he
was cross when he arrived to pick Doug up, and Doug was still upset
when he arrived in Albuquerque. Other than that, it worked out
fine. He enjoyed the snow, enjoyed reaching down and touching it.
I suppose it must have reminded him of the snow in Pennsylvania.

On Christmas Day David and Angi joined us for the opening of
presents and the ritual feast. The present Loren had driven through
snow to buy me turned out to be a bright red rolling suitcase—a very
festive piece of luggage. He always thinks of better presents for me
than I do for him. We had a fine, cozy day.

Having the first Christmas in a new house goes far toward making it a home.

THE FIRST FULL YEAR

January and February were a hibernating sort of time with quiet
hours of reading and writing and making soup. And then it was
March, and even though many of the migratory birds had already
headed back north, we decided to take an overnight trip to the
waterfowl refuge south of Albuquerque, the Bosque del Apache
National Wildlife Refuge, to look at those that were still there.

On the way, we drove through the town of Socorro and I had one of those moments that start you wondering about yourself. There is a small university in Socorro, and we were driving around the campus when I surprised myself by saying, without the slightest forethought, "Wonder if they could use a professor of engineering and a professor of English to fill in some semester?"

Loren swiveled in his seat to turn an amazed look at me. "Are you saying you wish you were back in the classroom?"

No, of course I didn't wish that. At least, I hadn't thought I did. Yet faced with a pleasant looking campus of humane size, my immediate impulse was to jump in. *I guess that's what it means, I wrote later, to have an identity. I guess it's going to take some time before I'm fully detached from students and semesters and grade sheets and firmly anchored in retirement, so I can really know who I am when I'm not working.*

I know a waterfowl refuge in the desert sounds like an anomaly, but there it was, and we were glad we went. We saw coots, sandhill cranes, snow geese, Canada geese, a snowy egret, various kinds of ducks, golden eagles—my new bird book came in handy. But I think I was every bit as fascinated by the water system as by the birds. First built by the Civilian Conservation Corps during the Depression and steadily improved since, the Bosque del Apache NWR takes water from the Rio Grande, circulates it through a system of canals and water-gated ditches to make ponds and swamps, then, after the birds have left, shifts it to the watering of grain fields to feed them the next year, and finally releases it back into the river downstream. Ingenious.

At sunset we watched the sandhill cranes fly back to their ponds from a day of foraging, then drove back to Socorro for the night. The next morning we drove on to White Sands, where we played in the snowy gypsum before heading home. We passed through towns with musical names: Alamogordo, Cloudcroft, Ruidoso, Carrizozo, Corona. So much variety in two days' drive! And still all those other drives waiting to be taken—to Silver City and the cliff dwellings, to Jemez and the great caldera, to Chama, to Chaco Canyon, to Taos

and the bridge over the Rio Grande gorge: all part of the adventure
I'd been referring to when people asked why we were retiring so
soon. There were ruins we wanted to climb, and we didn't want to
wait too long, I'd said. And we still meant to do all those things. Yet
now that we were here, it was at least equally pleasant to be in our
own quiet place and explore our own few acres.

During those early weeks of 2003 I fixated on TV news, watching the president walk us down the road to Iraq in much the same
way as I'd sat in front of the TV in a fit of depression when the first
President Bush went to war in Kuwait. This time it wasn't so much
depression as acute sadness. The images of that time stay with me.
Wolf Blitzer on CNN in khakis instead of his usual suit. Flashes of
night bombing in the sky over Baghdad. Iraqi soldiers searching
through reeds along the riverside for downed American pilots. All
that "shock and awe." A title occurred to me for a book I might
write: *The Older I Get the More I Cry*. No book to go with it, only a
title, but true enough. It finally became a poem.

I watched the screen and then went outside and walked around
and looked at our deep, peaceful sky. Peaceful, and yet I knew the eco-
nomic life of New Mexico was firmly tied to war: the air bases, Sandia
Labs, White Sands Missile Range, Los Alamos still at it ever since the
days of the Manhattan Project, the munitions rumored to be stashed
in tunnels in the Manzanos—those same Manzanos that I could see
from my front porch, with their bears, their deer, their Lost Maples.

*March 25. It's still plenty cool out, but there's no doubt,
spring is arriving. We aren't entirely glad. Our first winter seems
to have gone too fast. I'm feeling sorry to lose this first season of
muffled days indoors, multi-layers of clothes, and winter foods.
I'm going to miss seeing hard little pellets of snow in the air.*

Technically, this was our second spring in New Mexico, but it
felt like the first because we had been so involved with the building

of the house the year before that we hadn't quite noticed. We noticed now.

A friend who had recently moved to Mississippi sent me an email asking if spring was as lovely in New Mexico as it was there. I had to say I thought it probably wasn't. It was quite subdued. I began to see a few creeping plants with half-inch purplish blooms. Some of the cacti started budding, and if I looked close I could glimpse slivers of the fuchsia and yellow that would later flare open. Down in Albuquerque, daffodils bobbed beside the church door, and plum and peach trees threw open their blooms in people's yards. But it was a different bio-zone up where we lived, fourteen hundred feet higher than the city. Life was more austere. There wasn't much color. Our spring was beautiful in its way, but not lovely. We were too close to the bone for loveliness.

There on our stark ridge I felt close to the very structure of things. I had something of the same feeling when later that year we visited the Rock Church at Helsinki during a Baltic cruise. The Rock Church is a more or less round sanctuary blasted from solid granite. From the outside, all that is visible is the roof, a shallow copper bowl inverted on the grass. A walkway at the side of the bowl slopes downward to the door, opening into the earth itself. Inside, light comes from around the edges of the roof. It was a very moving, spiritual place. Clearly visible in the walls are the marks of the drilling for the dynamite. Like Christ's wounds, I thought. And the church itself called to mind the sacred kivas of New Mexico's pueblo people.

Our retirement was doing something of that same thing for us, I thought—bringing us closer to the earth itself, to all the rock-real, the authentic.

April 19. Heard mourning doves after breakfast. Hadn't known we even had them here. Heard them again this afternoon while out walking—such a soft, soothing sound. Might have missed it if not for the deep quiet all around.

Spring in a landscape close to the bone.

Though spring had started, it was slow in coming on, and once I had accepted the slipping away of our quiet winter I wanted it to hurry up. I was impatient to get the garden in.

We'd had Angus scrape off rocks and cactus from a relatively flat, open area uphill from the house to make a garden spot. It would obviously have been too hard for us to clear and dig up on our own. He brought in soil that he'd mixed himself, incorporating the cleanings of his corral, and moved in a used 2,500-gallon tank to store water. He set it securely in place on the high side of the garden and ran a line between it and the smaller tank buried at the base of our foundation, which caught roof water through the gutters and downspouts. A submerged pump with an automatic shutoff lifted the water to the storage tank, and from there we could water the garden by gravity flow. It was a beautiful system. With that and the absence of air conditioning, we could feel we were really living green.

We had intended to keep our piece of land as close to the way we found it as we could, but in fact we were altering it all the time. We had made deep wounds in it during the building process, with the pushing over of trees and breaking up of rock, the carving out and graveling of a driveway, the fastening of a foundation onto the land, the gouging out of a septic tank and leaching field and a trench

for running underground utility lines. Then the scraping and filling
of the garden, the alien soil we had Angus bring in, the marks of his
truck tires hauling it, the water tank visible from the road. And then
there were the lesser violations of the paths we wore with our rambling around and the plants I couldn't resist putting in, even though
we'd sworn we wouldn't have a lawn or flower beds.

The first of our plantings was the sweet clover I sowed on the
septic field soon after we moved in. Then, in the early fall, I put in a
little Russian olive tree at the base of the field, to screen it from the
road—an invasive plant not indigenous to the region that, as I later
read in the newspaper, environmentalists were trying to eradicate
from the area. Then I planted some iris by the front porch and, that
spring, some daylily corms I'd had waiting in the garage all winter.
When I got them out to put them in the ground, they had already
started putting out pale green shoots. I liked their eagerness to grow,
but these tender shoots made them prime targets for ground squirrels
and rabbits. Within two days, every little shoot had been gnawed off.
For a while the bulbs kept putting up more, but after being nipped
back every time they tried to sprout, they gave up and disappeared
into the soil.

The spear-like leaves of the iris were tougher. The iris corms
pushed them steadily up in spite of nips, and one, but only one that
first year, put up a flower stalk. Oh, how I watched over that one
stalk as it grew and budded! It had just two buds, one at the top and
one lower. Color began to show in the top one. Then finally one
morning I found that it had opened into a spectacular bloom, orchid
below, paler orchid above, with dull gold beards. By noon a strong
wind came up, so strong I was afraid the stalk would snap. I debated
whether to cut the one good bloom and bring it in, but if I did, the
other bud might not develop and open. I kept going to the nearest
window to check, and on one of those checks was just in time to see
a squirrel approach the stalk and rear up on its back legs. I was out
the door in a flash, clapping my hands and scolding. It ran off a few

yards and sat down with its back to me, making a great show of indif-
ference. I should have stood guard or else cut the flower right then.
Instead, I went back to my quilting, got sleepy, and leaned my head
back for a ten-minute nap. When I woke up, I at once thought of the
iris and rushed to the window to check. Gone! Completely gone—
both the open blossom and the bud! All that was left was a
chomped-off stalk.

*May 5. This is what I see as I sit at my computer and look
out the window. On the left, the pinkish-tan stucco of the garage
wall, like a frame for the dull-green piñon and juniper foliage at
the center and right, and an occasional bird in the big sky. If I
stand up I can see the snow peaks of the Sangre de Cristos. If I
turn and look over my right shoulder, out the dining room window and over the porch rail and beyond the bare space that hasn't
yet healed over from construction, there's a scattered array of
brush sloping down toward the road. If I stand up and walk to
that same window, I look out over the plains of the Estancia
Basin, with that pale orchidy shimmer of the earth dissolving into
pale blue at the horizon. To the south, the round foothills of the
Manzanos.*

*Loren's view from the window by his computer is straight out
that way, due south. He sees pieces of the winding downward
slope of our road clear to the interstate and beyond, toward the
Manzanos. It's a more spacious view than mine, but I wouldn't
say a better one. If he looks up from his work, he can see toy
trucks moving along the highway. He says seeing them makes him
feel close to the flow of this great American artery. If the wind is
from the south we can sometimes hear the hum of the traffic, just
faintly. I'm not as glad of it as he is.*

*From the back windows of the living room, breakfast room,
and our bedroom we look out at the upward slope toward the
crest of the ridge—almost like the ridge of a roof, it's that pro-*

nounced. If it weren't for this crest we would have a view of
Sandia Peak. Even so, the slope is a nice view in itself. I look out
at that green slope and think yes, our own place, right up to that
line of trees, there near the top.

Even into April, it was still too cold to plant the garden. I had
put in onion sets about the end of March, but was impatient to be
out doing more. A lot of days it was too muddy even to go walking.

Much as I enjoyed our peaceful quiet, out away from the city,
with elbow-room between us and our nearest neighbors, there were
days when it wasn't enough, and a fit of loneliness sometimes
descended on me like a dense cloud. It was especially hard to shake
that spring. Loren was shut off at his computer, finishing a book and
facing a deadline. I understood deadlines, of course, just as I understood getting too wound up in a piece of writing to leave it, deadline
or not. Nevertheless, I felt lonely, and went into "poor me" fits. Poor
me, indeed—while I cooked strip steaks for dinner and sipped my
wine and listened to bluegrass or Beethoven CDs!

One evening when I was especially down, Loren suggested a
walk after dinner. We set out up the road to the north in silence, but
when we reached the bend where we could see Sandia Peak I confessed that I was feeling lonely. It was unreasonable, I knew; only the
week before we had gone to an opera at UNM with friends, but so it
was. And as usual, the mere act of telling took the bad feeling away.
I was able to look around and enjoy the rapidly gathering dusk. It was
getting too dark to make the full mile-and-a-half loop, and we were
chilly. In the dim last daylight we came back into the house feeling
altogether more contented than when we'd left. Later, when we went
to bed, we lay close and enjoyed the envelope of night outside our
windows.

Still, I kept thinking why this loneliness? I was right where I wanted to be, with the person I wanted to be with. And I liked the quiet. Of course I did. But sometimes I needed people, and at those times the isolation grabbed me and twisted me around wrong.

May 16. A great abundance of purple and yellow wildflowers have popped up, and red blossoms have opened on some of what I like to call pin cushion cactus, really claret cup. Yesterday I saw some bright pink flowers growing low against the ground—small, only about five-eighths of an inch across, and such an intense pink they are almost fuchsia. Not a color I usually like much, but in this case, yes. Unlike the purple ones, which grow in masses, and the yellow ones in little clumps, these seem to live as solitary individuals, one here, one there, little separate pink faces looking up from the ground.

And today I planted some seeds: corn, beans, and squash—the big three.

I had persuaded myself that it was time to plant, but actually it wasn't. The cool weather dragged on. Nothing came up. I began to wonder if the large black beetles I was seeing in great numbers were eating my seeds underground.

These beetles were quite handsome, as beetles go, and had an amusing habit of standing on their heads when agitated, with their large rears up in the air. I'd never seen such a beetle before, but recognized it at once from Frank Cushing's book of Zuni folk tales, which I'd used once in a southwestern American literature course. As Cushing retells the traditional story, the beetle itself accounts for its habit of "kicking its heels into the air and thrusting its head into any crack or hole it finds" by claiming that it is listening to what's going on among the Holy People underground. And what the Holy People are saying now, the beetle explains when threatened by the coyote, is that someone is about to be in big trouble for desecrating their trail. The coyote thinks to himself, "I've been up and down this trail all day and have desecrated it several times"—and runs off. Thus does the clever tip beetle trick Coyote and escape being eaten.

Just before I left town for a conference, corn sprouts appeared and bean plants started pushing their sturdy necks above the ground. Things were growing at last! I rushed off to Parker's Nursery, nearby —a wonderful place that produced its own stock for local conditions—and brought home eggplant, tomato, and pepper plants, and even artichokes. I'd never even imagined growing artichokes, but when I asked Mr. Parker he said yes, artichokes did grow there in the East Mountains and I could expect to have some by the end of the summer. After I got all my plants in the ground, we caged the tomatoes and peppers, to protect them from our animal friends, since the garden wasn't yet fenced and Loren couldn't do anything about it until he got his book in. The eggplants and artichokes looked sturdy enough that I was confident they could fend for themselves, unprotected. Wrong. When I came back from my trip, I found only white plastic tags where the plants had been. Even the corn and bean sprouts had disappeared without a trace.

We had known that if we put in a garden we would have to expect to share with the deer and rabbits and ground squirrels. But somehow I had thought they would have the good sense to let things grow up and bear before they started dining on them. Not so. The hoofprints were plain to see.

Now, though, with his book off to the press, Loren was ready to turn his energies to fencing. Of course, the doctor had told him not to jolt his rheumatoid-damaged joints with hammering, but sometimes he isn't a very good listener.

It's hard to fence out deer, they're such jumpers. But he had read somewhere that they don't like to jump into a narrow space, so he designed a double fence, one a couple of feet inside the other. His design also provided bracing and cross-bracing to compensate for not setting the posts at an adequate depth, due to the rockiness of our ridge. The two fences essentially held each other up. I was greatly impressed. While he worked on it, I replanted, and this time put chicken-wire cages around the seedlings. Of course, as they grow beyond their cages, the tips become vulnerable to nibbling, and one promising little potato plant that I didn't bother to cage went into the ranks of the missing.

Probably it was the rabbits, more than the deer, who did this. Even onions got grazed off at ground level, those that weren't stepped on and mashed into the earth by deer hooves. But once the fence was finished, it did the trick, and when they were no longer getting chewed off as fast as they sprouted, things started growing. The tomato plants turned dark and bloomed and started setting fruit, the potatoes luxuriated, the squash sprawled, the green pepper plants churned out peppers, the eggplants made dusty-orchid blooms and then their beautiful glossy purple bulbous fruits (always better to look at than to eat). I even set out two grape-vines and two black-berry vines from Mr. Parker's nursery to spread on the inner chicken-wire fence, and positioned our soaker hoses to deliver precise little streams of water to them from the storage tank. They thrived and so did we.

The yuccas started blooming. First, fleshy red blobs pushed up from the middle of the plants—ungainly, bloody looking masses like some internal organ inappropriately displayed. Then, as if by mira-cle, these opened into stalks of milky white blossoms.

Summer also brought visitors. We showed them every detail of the house, tramped them around the lot, took them to the top of Sandia Peak and to the ruins at Bandelier—such an exciting place to have on one's doorstep. We kept meaning to extend our sightseeing to Chama, but put it off.

When Rick and his wife Tina came, we mentioned that we were thinking of buying the lot next to us on up the hill, another two-and-a-half acres. "You ought to," they urged. "You really should." David and Angi said the same. We kept looking at it, thinking about it. We

Angel helps Loren finish the garden fence.

did want to keep our feeling of space, and since both lots were shaped deep and narrow and our house sat toward one side, because the contour of the slope would have made it difficult to build at the center, a house on this next lot would likely mean people staring straight into our garage and master bath.

Someone had in fact started building something there and gone off and left it. We had seen the abandoned traces the day the real estate agent first brought us, and even then the remnants looked to have been there a long time—a garage-sized concrete slab, a few concrete blocks, scrap lumber curled up by the sun. Now the slab was littered with broken glass—from kids coming there to drink beer, neighbors said, and throwing their bottles when they finished. We also discovered a trash dump between two nearby junipers, with glass and rusted cans. Whoever had put in the slab must have been camping there. It was strange. I found a rusty bucket tossed under one of the junipers and used it for collecting the pieces and shards of glass I sporadically picked up. Every time it rained, the loose earth shifted a little and more pieces showed up, reflecting the sun.

We wondered if whoever had put the slab there might come back and start over. I made up my mind to investigate. It turned out to be easy. All I did was phone the county tax office and they gave me the name and address of the owners. Oddly enough, they lived in Texas, not many miles from where we'd been in Bryan. I wrote and asked if they might be interested in selling the lot. They might, they said, and gave a phone number. Loren and I talked it over, and I called the owners to talk about it. Were they the people who had put in the slab? I asked. No, they said, broken glass and all, it had been there when they bought the land. So we would never know. But when I made an offer, they accepted. That easily, we doubled the size of our land on the ridge to five acres, and at once stepped up our removal of glass and trash.

August. We had fresh-picked corn and tomatoes for lunch today, and there'll be more tomorrow. And by sticking a finger in under a potato plant I can break off beautiful little red-skinned new potatoes.

They were the first potatoes I'd ever grown. We also had such a bounteous supply of zucchini that I stockpiled zucchini chocolate cakes in the freezer. Artichokes, just a few scrawny ones.

September 19. So many rabbits! I wish Laura and Angel's kids were here to see them. They never saw a one when they were here. Yesterday there was a baby one grazing on the grass I planted last year just beyond the patio. It was maybe half as big as an adult but seemed much more alert to movement inside the windows than the grown ones are and quicker to startle. It ran when I made the slightest motion. You'd think time and experience of the world would teach them to be more apprehensive as they got older, not less.

That fall we decided to build a cactus-free trail around the perimeter of our five-acre spread. My job was digging out the cactus to clear the way. What proved most useful for this was not a shovel but a rake. Bracing it against the pads of a prickly pear or the bulk of a claret cup cactus, with the tines straddling the central stalk, I could exert a slow pull and bring it up from the ground with its long, hairy roots dangling. Great care was required then to keep the whole vicious mass balanced on the rake until I could deposit it on top of a more out-of-the way cactus or clump of yucca. Our land sprouted devil-piles of these uprooted cacti, held away from the soil by their fellows, drying in the sun.

Loren did the heavy work of wheelbarrowing wood chips to surface it, and Angi helped carry rocks to mark its sides through stretches where it might be hard to follow. The reward was a fine trail winding around the property, cushioned underfoot by the wood chips that also kept it from being muddy.

From that time on we were never at a loss for what to do with an empty half hour—we could always walk the trail. It offered a degree of variety and interest way out of proportion to its actual length, about a mile and a quarter. In some places it ran fairly level and open and in others wound up or down slopes, through woody patches and over rocks or even stone steps. But it never went through cactus. I had grubbed them out along the whole route, and Loren kept uprooting any little sprouts that tried to come back.

Even though we were always seeing the signs that deer were around, we saw the actual deer much less often than rabbits. For days we wouldn't see a one. Then two or three would come around the corner of the house and stand grazing just off our patio, or suddenly, silently, step out of the brush. There they would be, when we weren't even looking, then gone again. One morning when we were brushing our teeth, a couple of does suddenly appeared in the mirror above our heads. We turned and watched as they strolled past the end of the driveway, on up the slope toward the ridge. Sightings like this were always exciting—partly, of course, because they were so beautiful. When there was snow on the ground it became even easier to spot their hoofprints—lots of them—yet even after Loren bought a bale of hay at the feed store in Estancia and put it out on a clear spot a little way up the slope, which we could see from the back window in our bedroom, we rarely saw them. When we weren't looking, the hay disappeared by magic.

One day a doe looked in the window at Loren while he was working at his computer. It startled him, of course, that deer face just suddenly there with its nose practically pressed against the glass. Then he saw that there were three more with her. In as low a voice as possible, so as not to startle them, he called me to come see. After we had watched them for several minutes, they turned, all four together, and looked intently toward something beyond the corner of the house. We slipped away to the living room to look out another window and saw a coyote trotting up the slope, as oblivious to the deer as they had been attentive to him.

It was even more surprising when, not long afterward, Loren saw sheep peering through the window. Once again he called for me to come see. We hadn't been aware of any sheep anywhere around, but there they were, four of them, the same number as the deer. After a bit they made their way around the back corner of the house onto the patio, which they seemed inclined to take as their home away from home until I went out and shooed them away. At that, they dashed in a clump around the next corner, past the garage door, and partway down the driveway, then stood uncertainly for some time, as if wondering whether they didn't really want to make another try for the patio. Whether they finally went home on their own or were fetched, we never knew. It turned out they belonged to a muscled, suntanned woman who lived across the road from us and pretty much kept to herself—as did most of the folks there in the East Mountains.

It was some time that same fall, our second fall in the house, that
my email brought me a message that taught me something important. It was from a graduate student I'd known at Texas A&M. I had
been on her dissertation committee, but the topic proving overly
ambitious, she hadn't made much headway, and I had lost track of
her even before I retired. Now she was writing to say that she was
ready to get back to it and that she wanted me to continue serving
on the committee if I would be willing. Her topic was the kind I like,
heavy on historical content, so I wrote back to say yes, I'd be glad to.
I added that I'd wondered what became of her but had supposed I'd
simply been replaced on the committee. Or that's what I *meant* to
write. Instead, I wrote that I supposed I'd been "displaced."

When I realized the slip I'd made, I was taken aback. It didn't
seem like the kind of typo caused by careless fingers. Was I really, in
fact, feeling displaced? At some deep level did I feel I had landed
where I didn't belong—despite how happy I was, consciously, to be
there? I thought of the bluebonnet seeds that I'd scattered on our lot
several times, that hadn't come up—bluebonnets, the state flower of
Texas. Maybe those seeds were wiser than I was. Maybe they realized
they didn't belong in that unfamiliar soil. Or maybe they would yet,
in another year and with different weather conditions, sprout and
bloom.

Winter hushed everything again. Most days the weather was
bright and blue, but there were occasional precious days of soft gray
skies heralding snow that closed down around us and shut out all the
world beyond the closest trees. We lived, at those times, in a world
like a black and white photograph, the sky a gray fuzz, the ground
and tree branches all white fluff, punctuated with black trunks. We
ate slow-cooked soups and stews and looked out the windows.

And I quilted a lot. Since I both piece and quilt by hand, summer isn't the best time for it. Holding a big, stuffed quilt in one's lap

is hot! But for me, doing it that way is recreation; doing it on the sewing machine would be work. Also, it's quiet that way—literally quiet, noiseless. All winter long, I alternated between finishing a book about war poetry and quilting like a fiend.

I can never decide whether I enjoy the piecing or the quilting more. The quilting is usually considered the part where a person shows her skill as a needlewoman. But piecing has the advantage of filling me with the junctions of colors, whether a small number of repeating colors, as in a planned quilt, or the random encounters of a scrap quilt.

Sometimes I'm seized by a vision of a particular color combination that simply compels me to plan out a quilt and go to the fabric store. Even if I find what I'm looking for, of course, the outcome is never certain. After the most careful planning and shopping and all the work that goes into the making of it, the finished product may fail to live up to my vision. Or it may exceed the expectation—that's happened too. The summer we were building the house, I made a quilt for Beka using several yards of a light lavender and a pale green that I'd bought without anything in particular in mind, just because they were on sale and I liked them. Along with those two, I used a dark purplish print left over from another project. Since I had only so much of each and probably couldn't buy more, it took a good deal of effort to figure out a pattern that would use them in such a way as to make a whole quilt, but it was worth the effort because I was so sure the colors would be good together. When I finished the piecing, I was disappointed. The total effect struck me as uninteresting, lacking in subtlety. But at that point there was nothing to do but go ahead and quilt it. I quilted *and quilted* (it was a big queen-size spread) and after I was finished it was so pretty I could hardly bear to part with it. The quilting, by adding depth, had restored the richness I'd imagined when I chose to combine the purple and the green. But it could just as well have gone the other way and been the disappointment I first judged it to be. I don't seem to have a very accurate anticipatory eye.

The flower basket quilt that kept growing.

Before we retired, there were days when I would so wish I could stay home and quilt. That first couple of years of retirement, I caught up with my pent-up urge. Besides Rebekah's big quilt, I made four crib quilts, a queen-size spread from a pattern I'd seen at Ketchikan once when we took an Alaskan cruise, twin-size spreads for two of the granddaughters, a bear paw for our granddaughter Melissa, a flower-basket quilt with diagonal sets that I miscalculated so it came out king size instead of queen and went to Laura and Angel instead of to us, a flower-and-wreath spread for David and Angi, a scrap star quilt, and my favorite of favorites, a scrap double Irish chain in clear greens and blues on white. It's on the bed in our front guest room today, with a Georgia O'Keeffe poster in those same colors hanging above it. All those quilts in just two years.

The second week in December, we went with a small tour group to Zuni, in far western New Mexico, to attend the Zunis' Shalako ceremony, or that portion of it that they had re-opened to outsiders.

The Zunis have an elaborate year-long ceremonial calendar that culminates in December with the return of the Shalakos, delegates from the gods living at the bottom of a nearby lake. The Shalakos are represented during the ceremony by huge, brightly painted effigies made of wood and leather, in the form of great birds. They enter the village at a certain time every year, at a certain point along a dry creek south of the village, and the very sacred story of the people's emergence and migration is retold. It is this part of the annual ceremonial that is closed to all but the Zunis themselves. Then the Shalakos begin dancing in the houses, one to each kiva or clan that has been selected for that year's special blessing. For a number of years the dancing too had been closed to outsiders, but now a limited number are allowed to come and watch.

At the chosen houses, either a special room will have been built, with an extra high ceiling, or a trench will have been dug down the middle of the main room to accommodate the Shalako figure's great height. Spectators sit along the sides of the room, and men from that kiva who are expert drummers are grouped at the end. Animal heads mounted around the walls have been ornamented with turquoise necklaces and forehead pieces. This is the Zunis' way to show their gratitude for the animals who have given their lives. The animals seem to stare back their gratification.

From midnight until six in the morning we stood outside the windows of the six houses, one after the other, looking in as these strange yet beautiful birdlike figures, one to each house, danced up and down to the intricate drumming. And oh, when they clacked their wooden beaks and swooped down the whole length of the trench, before dancing their way back! At one house, toward morning, after the crowd had thinned out, we went inside to get warm and were served bowls of hot stew—because at Shalako, all visitors are to be fed. We also had the privilege of seeing the Mudheads, a small number of nearly naked tribal members who go from one designated house to another, representing the earliest humans, misshapen and ill-behaved due to their having been the products of incest between the son and daughter of the Sun Father and the Earth Mother. The Mudheads' shenanigans are always comical and crude, since they come from a time before the human race learned to behave, but the Mudheads themselves are regarded as being very sacred, from being so close to the origin of all things, so close to the creator gods.

How wonderful it was, we felt, to live so near these mysteries, though we understood them so poorly. For hundreds of years the Shalakos, representing the Council of the Gods, have appeared annually at that certain point along that certain creek and have danced for their people. Theologically, what a profound idea—that the gods are faithful and reliable, that the divine can be counted on to keep coming back into human life, world without end, amen.

And then came Christmas, and another re-entry of the divine.

We didn't care to risk a repetition of Doug's Christmas trip the previous year. Instead, a few days before Christmas, we loaded up our presents for all the Texas children and grandchildren and set forth. We picked up Doug and his clothes and his medicines in Fort Worth and then drove a huge loop around the state, making stops in Houston, League City, and Austin to visit and leave off presents. After a while we began to feel that we should just slow down, say ho-ho-ho, and toss out the goodies.

When we finished the last delivery, we headed back to New Mexico. On Christmas Eve, we arrived home to the tree we had left all decorated, with presents underneath, having driven something like two thousand miles in four days. A couple of days after Christmas, off we went again to take Doug back, another twelve-hundred-mile round trip. It was exhausting—over three thousand miles in little over a week—but we couldn't very well make his visits longer because he gets bored and uneasy if he's away from his own routine for more than a few days. We certainly weren't going to leave him to his own devices at Christmas. So it appeared this was going to be an annual routine. But I began to wonder how long we could keep it up.

2004, Our Third Year

For New Year's, friends from College Station drove out and met us at Socorro, and we went out to the shallow lagoon at the bird refuge before daylight and watched the cranes and geese wake up and take off for their day's foraging. There was a thin sheet of ice on the water, and as the sun came up it glazed over with a rose-colored sheen. Another of those moments one remembers.

More days of cocooning.

At the end of February we drove to Tucson to hear our wonderful daughter-in-law Tina play a piano quintet in the chamber music festival there. We walked around the desert museum in the winter sun, toured San Xavier del Bac Mission with Tina's mother and sister and brother-in-law, then swelled with pride at the concert itself as she simply took charge of Cesar Franck's big, difficult music.

On our way back the bright desert weather turned nasty with fog, heavy rain, and intermittent snow. We debated whether it was prudent to stop off in Albuquerque for a committee meeting at church, as we'd planned, but told ourselves the heavy weather was lightening up, it would be OK. But when we came out it was still raining. And when we got up into Tijeras Pass the rain turned to heavy snow, coming down thick. It was impossible to see more than a few feet ahead. There we were, on a scary enough stretch of interstate at best, with big rigs all around us, no visibility, and everybody at risk of skidding out of control. So when we came to an exit onto the side road, the old Highway 66, we took it. What a mistake that was! At least on the interstate there were snow-plows and lights and the lanes were marked. Off on the side road there was nothing—just the sharp drop-offs that we knew were there along the side but couldn't see. I put on my leather gloves so if we went off the road and were thrown out of the car I wouldn't be skidding along on bare skin.

Loren held us to a creep. Oh, how thankful we were to get home!

In the spring, only a few weeks after that late snow, Beth and Roy came again. Off we went to Silver City, down in the southwestern corner of the state, stayed the night at a bed and breakfast, and came back by way of the Gila cliff dwellings, where they boldly climbed rickety ladders up to the recessed rock rooms while I stayed on the trail. Crossing the Plains of San Agustin, west of Socorro, we stopped and toured the Very Large Array, an installation of twenty-seven giant radio antennae silently surveying space. Not being the slightest bit of a physicist, I hadn't particularly cared to stop and see it; I had imagined it would be boring. Not so! As we left, I thought—not for the first time—what a state this was that we had chosen for our retirement. And we still hadn't visited Chama. In fact, the four of us talked about maybe driving up there the next day, but we were tired of being in the car. Instead, we spent the last day at home, playing Scrabble®, drinking tea, looking out the windows.

> *June 25. The birds have come back. We had a great influx of them two or three months ago—piñon jays, western scrub jays, a few robins, juncos. So many they could empty out the feeder in two days. Then they all seemed to go away. Last month we saw hardly any birds at all. This morning I heard bird calls as the sun came up, and there they were at the feeder again. A black-headed grosbeak, I think it is, has been singing splendidly for us, elaborate runs and trills. Jays are hanging around, and now some newcomer with a rose-washed face and bib has turned up—I think a Cassin's finch, after consulting the bird book. Earlier this afternoon, driving home from the feed and seed store in Estancia, I saw a hawk beside the road—maybe a red-tailed hawk, I'm not sure. I had to keep my eyes on the road.*

Yes, I was indeed learning to be retired.

In many ways this was our most wonderful summer. Yet things kept happening, problems kept popping up that at the time seemed like only small interruptions of our good days, but in retrospect look very much like warnings. I think this was the summer when we first clearly realized that we were getting old.

We gardened, we had friends to dinner, we went to their houses for dinner. I went around soliciting donations for the art auction at church—a new experience that meant summoning up my nerve.

Steven came to visit, and we drove to the Great Caldera and to Bandelier National Monument, and this time I went into the gift shop and bought a copy of Adolf Bandelier's novel about native life in that place that his name is attached to. Friends from Texas A&M, David and Mary Ann, came to visit, and we drank fresh watermelon juice in the café on the square at Santa Fe and Loren took them to Bandelier while I stayed home with a sick stomach. Laura and Angel and the children came, and we drove up to the high country at the Colorado border and took a day-long excursion on the Cumbres and Toltec Scenic Railroad. We camped two nights at the edge of a fast stream, very beautiful, though plagued with mosquitoes when the sun started going down, and so cold we were grateful to Angel, campfire lover that he is, for keeping a fire going and plying us with hot coffee. But delightful as it was to be with them, we found that we didn't honestly enjoy the camping itself. We were in our familiar little pop-up camper that we had pulled behind the car for years, in which we'd enjoyed so many trips. But now the step up from the ground seemed higher than it used to and the plywood under our sleeping bags harder. We came home feeling that our camping days were over.

As summer went on, the weather became too hot for quilting. It was just as well. My right hand was almost beyond use with arthritis. Same with the piano. I had thought that when we retired I would get back to serious playing—scales, working up a selected program of pieces, the whole thing. But the hands weren't up to it anymore. After fifteen minutes at the keyboard, they hurt and my back hurt, and my ears hurt worst of all. My days of playing fairly well seemed to be over too. I spent more and more of my time reading, writing, and walking our trail.

Loren was also having problems that summer. The knee that had had the Baker's cyst when we were moving into the house went bad, to the point that he had to use a cane, and one shoulder and arm developed pain and tingling from disk problems. He went for physi-

*With Loren, Elias, Celeste, and Laura, enjoying what was probably
our last time to camp out.*

cal therapy, to try to avoid surgery, then had surgery for a kidney
stone. The cataract his ophthalmologist had been watching reached
the point of needing surgery. Meanwhile, an unexplained pain that
had been stabbing my right hip for years got sharply worse. All this
in one summer.

We were greatly occupied, too, with the business of our property
owners association. I had been elected first vice-president, but shortly
afterward the president quit, leaving me to wear those shoes. At the
same membership meeting, Loren had been elected second vice-
president. and chair of the roads committee.

Our road was a major problem. Dirt with ditches on the side and
an uncertain covering of gravel, it turned into a slimy bog with the
least rain or snow. The one steepest slope was constantly washboarded. In dry weather—which thankfully was most of the time—
it generated billows of dust. We hadn't given much thought to what
it would be like to live on an unpaved road when we bought our lot,
but we had learned. I hated that road more every day that passed,
but until we became officers in the association I'd tried not to mention it more than, say, every other day, for fear of having Loren worry

that I wasn't happy with our choice. Now, charged with our new responsibilities, we confronted the fact that if we had it to do again, we wouldn't buy on an unpaved road with no county maintenance. While we studied our association's finances and tried to figure out a way to get the road paved, at least to the top of the washboarded hill, he poured time and physical labor into projects like digging out silted-up culverts. It didn't help my good cheer any that while he grubbed in the dirt other residents waved and kept going.

Aside from that damn road, though, and in the intervals between health problems, we were enjoying our work that summer. The book on war poetry that had occupied me since retirement had now gone to press, and I could turn my attention to another project I'd had in mind for some time, on women writers and artists of the Southwest. Never before had my work been so directly grounded in place—and my own place at that. From poring over reproductions of paintings and the illustrations of old books about the Southwest, I could look up at the picture outside my own window and there it was, the very thing! And Loren was also getting into some new research—always a happy time.

As the summer wore on, we sometimes spoke of driving into the city for a baseball game. When we bought our lot, the Dukes had still been playing in Albuquerque, and we had thought the idea of going to games on cool summer evenings, in a lower-key environment than at a major league ballpark, sounded like fun. But the Dukes folded before we even got moved. Then the Marlins organization decided that if Albuquerque would pony up for a new park, it would move its AAA team from Calgary. All during the summer of 2002, while our house was being built, the new ballpark was under construction too, and we followed its progress in the newspaper along with the controversy over a new name for the team. (It turned out to be the Isotopes: probably the only team in baseball history named for a joke in a TV series.). We told ourselves we were certainly going to go to games once they got the franchise going. And then they did. But somehow we never went. It wasn't as though I wouldn't have enjoyed it. It was just that the drive down through the canyon into the city always seemed like too much of a bother. We were happier staying home.

I've loved baseball all my life. When I was growing up in Fort Worth, I followed the Cats, in the AA Texas League, and Mother and Dad and I went to games at LaGrave Field. I remember Mother's displeasure that they sold beer at the games, and her shock when she discovered that people actually paid more for it than for soft drinks. I remember being there when some of the players got married at home plate. Bobby Bragan was the manager in those years, a fine catcher and a name of solid respect in the Dodgers organization. Dick Williams played center, and I think (or did I only imagine it?) had a certain aura of the fast life about him. And oh, Chico Carasquel, Wally Fiala, where did you disappear to? I remember Mother, who spoke no Spanish, holding onto Carasquel, who spoke no English, outside the dressing room after the game one night until I could finish getting someone else's autograph and scoot over for his. He went on to play some good shortstop for I think it was the White Sox.

Maybe I got my baseball interest from Granny. She was a big fan. When I spent Friday nights and Saturdays with her at her little two-room apartment with a shared bathroom down the hall, we listened to the games on the radio. Oh how we debated whether the name of the Phillies' Richie Ashburn should be pronounced rich-y or rick-y! I knew it was rich-y, but she always maintained the contrary, if only for the sake of argument. It seemed to me as though the World Series was always between the Dodgers and the Yankees in those years, and she was a big Dodgers fan, a Yankees hater in the best of the tradition. It used to irritate her beyond measure the way the Yankees kept winning the series. Funny, I don't remember a thing about her reaction when the Dodgers finally won in 1955. I was in high school by then.

I hadn't thought about all this in years until recently I happened
to watch part of the Ken Burns series on baseball and picked it up at
the segment that covered the late forties and fifties. It brought back
my Friday nights with Granny by the radio. I would like to believe
that one of these days I would find myself in a place called Heaven
and bump into her there. "So," I would say, "how did you like that
World Series back in '55?"

*August 10. This is supposed to be the monsoon season, but
very little rain so far. Gray-black clouds swirl up every afternoon
and it looks like we're going to get storms, but then most days all
we get is wind. The clouds just drift off after a little growling. If
this is all monsoon season is going to deliver, we're in for an even
worse wildfire season than the last couple of years.*

Actually, I liked the New Mexico wind. There was nearly always
this movement in the air, as if it were alive and darting around, taking an interest in things. It could get tiresome, of course, when a
strong blow went on day after day and all the windows and cars got
caked with dust and your skin felt gritty and your mouth tasted of it.
Our house whistled when the wind blew—a pleasant sound in mod-
eration, but not when it rose to a shrill whine.

Naturally, the wind added to the fire danger. We had not been
comfortable when someone who knew where we were renting during
the building of our house said, "Oh yeah, that house at the top of the
chimney." If a fire got started at the bottom of that cliff, he went on,
it would be at the top before we could back the car out. Great.

There had been a fire about five miles from us one afternoon the
summer we moved into our house that closed both sides of the interstate for a while and blocked some people from getting to their
homes. We could see the smoke from our patio, and when we walked
a little way and stood at the top of the hill we could see the flames
in the dry grass. It was not comfortable when the wind came up dur-

ing those months of drought. I kept thinking how fast a spark could spread and remembering that there were only two ways out of our subdivision, one of which was nearly impassable.

I began to be just slightly afraid in this place we had chosen for our retirement. We had speculated about what we would do if either of us encountered a bear while we were up at the garden. Now I began to look over my shoulder when I walked the trail. A mountain lion had been killed only three or four miles from us.

And then there were prowlers in the night.

We were both sound asleep when I suddenly became aware of voices outside, not right outside the window, but a few yards up the slope toward the ridge, close enough that I could hear their words. I sat bolt upright, startling Loren, who roused more slowly and sat up beside me.

"What's the matter?" he mumbled.

"Someone's out there."

We listened hard. Nothing. After a while we lay back down, and he went back to sleep—or I thought he did. I lay awake on the edge of the bed, tense and listening. And then I was sure I heard a gunshot. But still I didn't get up or say anything, just lay there listening for more until finally I went back to sleep.

The next morning neither of us said a word about the sounds in the night. I'm not sure why. Maybe we both felt that speaking of it would make it real, and we preferred to think we had imagined it. Days passed. Finally, at lunch one day, Loren broke the silence and asked what it was that had startled me awake the other night when I thought someone was outside. "Voices," I told him. "I heard people talking."

"I heard something too," he admitted. "Before you sat up, it was like I was hearing something in my sleep. I couldn't have said it was voices."

So then I acknowledged the rest. "After you went back to sleep, I heard a gunshot."

The gate.

"I wasn't asleep," he said. "I heard it too."

We'd already had a burglary, not long after we moved in. And during a heavy snowstorm the previous winter, one night about ten o'clock when the road was so deep in snow that no one was out, a guy had come to our door claiming to be looking for a friend. I didn't trust him a bit. When he knocked again and said his car was stuck in our driveway, and Loren went down to try to help get it out, I followed with an oversized flashlight that might serve as a weapon and a pencil and paper and wrote down the license number, and the woman with him didn't like it. Now this.

"I've hated to say so," I confessed, "but when you're out of town I'm uneasy staying here alone."

That very week he put in a strong iron gate across the driveway, with a chain and padlock, so at least intruders couldn't get a car in. Any time he was gone, after that, I closed and locked the gate, and felt somewhat better. But never quite the same.

CHAPTER NINE

People Are More Important

$\mathcal{I}$N 1912, the now revered, but then only aspiring, American novelist Willa Cather made her first visit to the Southwest. Her brother was stationed in Prescott, Arizona, with the Santa Fe Railway, and she went for a long visit with him, hoping to rest up from a hectic six years as editor at *McClure's Magazine* and to find a new direction for her life. While she was there, she did a lot of traveling around—to the Grand Canyon, to the Painted Desert, to Albuquerque—and as she did so she fell in love, not with a person but with the Southwest itself. We know this from the lively series of letters she wrote back to a friend in New York, Elizabeth Shepley Sergeant. In letter after letter she extolled the vastness of the place, its colors, the tang in the air. She especially loved the country around Albuquerque—loved it so much that she thought she would be able to write there: for Cather, a prerequisite to being able to live there. Then, abruptly, she wrote Sergeant that she was coming back east. She said she had realized that after all, people are more important than scenery.

That was one of the things Loren and I also learned in the Southwest. We were living in the very country Cather was talking about, and we too had fallen in love with it. Like Cather, we savored the sweeping vistas, the tones of earth and sky, the taste of the air. We loved its slopes and its rocks and its tip beetles and claret cup cactus. We had found a particular clump of juniper toward the back of our own five acres where deer liked to hide away and had seen the scuffed earth of their mating season. We had learned, from the quiet of the place, how to be retired. We fully intended to live on that rocky, prickly ridge embraced by New Mexico's horizon for the rest of our lives. But we came to realize that people are more important. In our case it was a particular person with particular needs for whom we were responsible, and we too went back east, though only as far as Texas.

The summer of 2004 was a time of worrying and fretting about prowlers, the threat of wildfire, bears, and health issues. But mainly I worried about Doug and whether we were fulfilling our responsibility to him. We had told ourselves that moving to New Mexico wouldn't be a problem; without a work schedule to limit when we could go and come, we would see him at least as often as we had been, maybe more. We could drive to Fort Worth every month or six weeks if we wanted to. After all, it was an easy drive, just a straight shot down I-40 and U. S. 287. And certainly it would be as easy for him to fly to Albuquerque as to College Station; he would be on bigger planes.

Our confidence sustained its first big crack when the call came, before we even got our foundation in, telling us that the place he had lived for the last fifteen years was closing. True, the new place we found for him after we got over the initial panic was an improvement. But the crack was still there. My assurance was no longer intact.

Then we learned that along with the old residential facility, he was losing the services of the social worker who had reliably facilitated his travel for so many years. No worry, we told ourselves; my bachelor brother had lived in Fort Worth all his life, and would surely be willing to take Doug to the airport and meet him if we were careful about scheduling. But then, less than three months after we moved into our house, Kenny married and moved to Seattle. That meant having to negotiate with Doug's father to take him to the airport for his Christmas trip and meet him coming back, and after trying it once I said never again. But I knew that with no more travel, Doug's world, already narrow enough, would narrow even further. We couldn't let that happen.

The next big crack in our system took us longer to see. Only after we had been at our new home for a year or so did we recognize that our leave-it-to-impulse approach wasn't getting us to Fort Worth as often as we ought to be going. Time had a way of slipping past. That seemed like an easy enough problem to resolve. We set ourselves what we thought was a realistic schedule—visit Doug every other month—and put it on the calendar in red. And for a while we adhered to it fairly well. But by the summer of 2004 other big cracks were opening up.

For one, I was having to ask myself how long we were going to be able to keep it up. Twelve-hundred-mile round trips were getting more tiring all the time. Yet even if we did manage to maintain our schedule of bimonthly visits, the truth was, it wasn't enough. He needed more.

I lay awake nights thinking about it. My confidence that we could look out for Doug from a distance of six hundred miles wasn't just cracked, it was shattered all to pieces.

That fall, when Loren was out of town one Sunday, I went to the front of the church during a prayer request time, knelt on the chancel steps, and whispered to Reverend Hammond that I needed help with a hard decision. "I'm not doing as much as I should for Doug and yet what we're doing is wearing us out, both of us. I'm thinking we need to move back."

He whispered back, "We need to talk."

When we found a chance to do so, he urged me not to do it. "You'll only get him more dependent on you than he already is," he said, "and make it harder for him when you die."

But actually, there was no reason to believe Doug would outlive us. People with brain trauma often have a shortened life span, and we could see him slipping all the time, as if going through a speeded-up aging process. All the more reason, then, to do what we could for him now.

I still had not mentioned all this to Loren. I kept putting it off, knowing what a hard blow it would be.

Our third and last Thanksgiving in our New Mexico house, which we had hung so much emotional baggage on and been so intent on living in it to the end, is only a blur. My mind was in knots, pulled in multiple directions as I tried to sort out my own sense of what we needed to do and my dread of opening the subject with Loren. I remember that we spent part of the day helping with our church's open-door feast for all comers. Letting others handle the serving line in the church hall, we drove around taking turkey dinners to shut-ins and giving them to street people, then hurried back home to make a late dinner of our own. I don't remember whether David and Angi came that year, but I do remember three very special unexpected guests.

I was spreading the tablecloth to start setting the table when I glanced out the window and saw three young stags, all with nice little racks of antlers, strolling up our gravel walk from the driveway. As they neared the steps to the front porch, as if planning to ring the doorbell, they veered off into the planting strip between the walk and the porch rail and started cropping the tops of the Russian sage and other plants that had grown there during the summer. When I moved closer to the window, they lifted their heads and stared at me for a moment, then, almost with a shrug, went back to their browsing. Three bachelors hired to do the weeding and intent on getting on with their work. The house and I were nothing more than parts of their landscape. As much as any other single image, the picture of those three beautiful antlered deer almost on our front porch epitomizes for me our life at Cerro Espinoso.

A few days after Thanksgiving I finally, sadly, shared with Loren the problem that was troubling me—that even though I wanted to stay here in the home we had planned, I was feeling that we needed to move back closer to Doug.

It was fully as hard as I had expected. He looked stricken. I believe he actually went pale. He had so loved this place that we had chosen out of all other possibilities and this house that he had planned and poured so much work into. I believe he loved the very ground itself. He wanted to stay where we were as long as we lived— as did I.

"I need some time to think," he said.

For several days we spoke very little, about this or anything else. He never berated me. He never asked how I could even think of such a thing. He was just very quiet. He would ask me a question now and then—how long had I been thinking about this, what had led me to it. I would reply as briefly as I could and go on about my reading, my quilting, whatever. I knew that when he was ready to talk it through, he would.

And when the time came, he said yes, I was right, we needed to go.

We both knew that telling David and Angi was going to be very hard. The four of us had been very close these past years, and Angi, whose relationship with her own father had been intermittent at best, was especially close to Loren. They had loved our place on the ridge, had loved driving out from town and rambling around with us. Moreover, they were now expecting a baby, and David very much wanted to see his son grow up in and out of his grandparents' house. He had even spoken of maybe finding a place of their own near ours, maybe just down the road, so their boy could come back and forth. It was an old-fashioned sort of fantasy, but a fine and loving one, and we were going to be ruining it.

We asked them to come out to dinner, and while we were sitting at the table, after everyone had finished, we told them we were leaving. Angi dropped her head onto Loren's shoulder and cried. I knew she felt that she was again being deserted by a father.

"Move Doug out here!" David urged. Friends at church—very dear friends by now—had said the same. But it would have been cruel to make him have to learn his way around another new place and have to give up his job that he took such pride in and lose the daily companionship of people he had known since school days. We tried to explain. We knew they wanted us to be there, near them, and we were glad they did. We wanted it too. But Doug needed us.

"We need you too!" Angi insisted.

"But not as much as he does."

I don't remember if it was then or later that Loren summed it up perfectly: "Doug is our one remaining real responsibility."

When I launched this big disruption of our lives by sharing my feelings of worry and, yes, guilt, I was assuming we would move to Fort Worth. That was where Doug was after all, and he was the reason for our going. Besides, Fort Worth was my first home, where I had started out in life. Memories clustered there were coming back thicker and faster as I got older. The house my grandfather built might be gone, and the spooky old multi-story Victorian on Henderson Street where I'd had piano lessons might have been long since torn down, but I still felt a stirring of pride when I drove east into the shambles that Rosedale Avenue had become and saw my beautiful old high school standing proudly up on its high bluff. I had pointed out to Loren, on one of our trips, the brick and stone portals on Forest Park Boulevard that had looked so massive to me—like a castle!—when Mother and Daddy took me to the zoo as a child, and the place on Vickery where I parked when I went to help Granny move out of her last little tacky apartment. Things like this are what it means to feel one's roots.

Actually, I didn't so much assume we would move to Fort Worth as wish to. But Loren's overriding preference was for a rural or small-town location. He stated it quite clearly when agreeing we should go: "I don't want to live in the city." After his graciousness in agreeing to give up our home and move again for the sake of, after all, his stepson, how could I not put his wishes first on this point? Not that I didn't recognize the appeal of the small-town life too. Besides, we both knew that if we were *too* close to Doug we would indeed make him more and more dependent. Even in New Mexico I got phone calls from him like "I can't find my stamps." Six hundred miles away, and I was supposed to tell him where his stamps were? If we lived just down the street or even just across town I would be running over there to help find things all the time.

The trouble was, there are a lot of small towns in that part of Texas, and for all we knew about any of them we might as well have put a map up on the wall and played Pin the Tail on the Donkey. We looked at their names and wondered where to start. Was there any chance at all that the climate would be a little cooler in one than in another? I did exhaustive Internet searches of weather records. No, of course there wasn't. Then one of us said, "Remember that little town where we took Beka's kids to the drive-through animal park last summer?" Oh yes, Glen Rose. It seemed like a nice little town.

So with scarcely more thought than that we got in touch with a real estate agent in Glen Rose and agreed to spend the twenty-eighth, three days after Christmas, looking at property.

I believe it was the fact of having made that appointment that made it seem real. We were really going to leave this place. We were really going to become transients again. Everything was changed. The special things about our house that I was so fond of had become commodities, mere assets.

Christmas season arrived, and we put out our chili pepper lights again on the big rocks flanking the entrance to the driveway and put up our tree. Once again we drove through Tucumcari, Amarillo, and Wichita Falls to Fort Worth and picked Doug up for the holiday, and once again made the big loop by League City and Houston and Katy and Austin to deliver presents before heading back to New Mexico. And once again were worn out when we got home, but happy to be there.

We exchanged our presents and ate our special foods and listened to CD after CD of holiday music. Then on the twenty-seventh we drove back to Fort Worth and delivered Doug to his residence. We spent the night at a motel at the south edge of town, and early the next morning we drove to Glen Rose to meet the real estate agent. She turned out to be not only pleasant and knowledgeable but remarkably well organized. To help us keep our bearings she had marked on a map the itinerary of houses and lots that we were going to look at, and she gave us color print-outs of all the listing sheets to refer to as we went. Yes, not just lots but houses too, because we had told ourselves maybe it didn't make sense to build this time. In truth, though, that was what we really wanted to do: build again and in fact, build our same house again. So we looked at both lots and existing houses, trying to convince ourselves to be sensible.

Stop number one marked on the map was a lot at the edge of town, or actually a strip of six lots, a little over an acre each, sitting side by side, covered with brush. Some of them more, some less, commanded a view of an empty, rolling expanse clear to the eastern horizon. No one would claim it looked like New Mexico; there weren't any crags or snow peaks. But it did have a hilly and spacious look, plus the advantages of being within the city limits ("city" meaning all of two thousand people)—water, sewer service, a more or less paved street. These, along with an out-in-the-country sort of feeling. "We might be interested in this one," we both said, and wrote some comments of our own on the listing sheet.

At the end of the tour, we hadn't seen any existing houses we cared to think further about. But we had found another piece of land that we were interested in, five acres west of town with an even better view of a hilly far horizon. This one didn't offer city utilities, however; we would have to put in a septic system and a well. And there was also the fact that it sided directly on a U. S. highway. We wondered if there would be an issue of traffic noise, and maybe safety considerations, from having to turn into the subdivision off a highway without any left-turn lane. Probably not, we told ourselves. It was only a two-lane highway and didn't appear to carry much traffic.

It was very quiet as we got out of the realtor's car and walked around. Hmm. We asked if she would please drive us back by the first lot so we could compare them.

We had an appointment with a realtor in Weatherford the next day, thinking we ought to be prudent and consider more than one area before deciding. We had thought we might drive on up that night. Fortunately, though, as it turned out, we were so tired after our day of looking that we decided to spend the night in Glen Rose and drive to Weatherford the next morning. Our motel, the only modern motel in town at the time, fronted on U. S. 67, the same highway that ran beside the five-acre lot. All night long we heard truck noise. The lot on the highway was out.

Weatherford is larger than Glen Rose—most places are—and not only closer to Fort Worth, but a straight shot down I-30, making it an ideal location for a bedroom community. And that is exactly what the past couple of decades had done to what used to be a quiet little country town with a splendid old courthouse. My mother and dad used to come to Weatherford to buy peaches and watermelons at the farmers' market. They wouldn't have bothered now, with all the traffic problems and farmland turning into subdivisions. We couldn't get out of there fast enough.

On the way home, driving those familiar miles yet again, we talked about what we had seen. The only house in either town that appealed to us had two fatal disadvantages: it was in a gated equestrian development, not exactly the real us, and it was two stories. Face it, we said, we weren't going to be climbing stairs very well for many more years. We kept coming back to the strip of brushy land at the edge of Glen Rose. The approach was up a rather steep hill until, as you crested it, you saw a distant prospect of rolling country spread out to a far horizon.

"We could buy two of the lots," I suggested. "Just like where we are, have two lots side by side."

"Or we could buy three," Loren answered.

Throughout our marriage, we have always done some of our best talking in the car.

An hour or so passed, time enough for me to think of a drawback.

"If we buy in Glen Rose, we'd have an hour of highway driving into Fort Worth. It may not be too many years before that gets hard. We didn't think the ten hours from the East Mountains was going to be hard either, and look how we feel about it now. We might wind up having to move again."

He pondered that only briefly. "If you want to be sure we won't ever have to move again," he replied, "we can just go on into a nursing home right now."

Oh. Yes. Once again he had put his finger right on it. I let go of worrying about the potential one-hour drive. We would take things as they came.

Within a week we made an offer on the three lots. We had bought another site for making a home.

We weren't going to move, of course, until we sold our house in New Mexico, and we had several things to do first. In late January Loren had cataract surgery, and in February we went on a long-planned South American cruise with friends from church. I was scheduled to have reconstructive surgery on my right thumb-wrist joint in mid-March. So we decided to wait and put the house on the market April first. That would give me two weeks for healing before lookers started coming through.

In the meantime, we sorted through our belongings for things to get rid of. One of those was the camper. We placed an ad in the Albuquerque newspaper.

The day the ad came out, the day before my scheduled surgery, it started snowing. When a pleasant-sounding man called and wanted to come out right then to look at the camper, we had to tell him maybe he should wait, the roads might be getting bad. He insisted he could make it. And he did. He took one look at the camper and

Our land in Glen Rose as it was when we first saw it.

bought it on the spot, giving us two hundred-dollar bills to hold it, and he would come back Saturday to give us the rest and pick it up. Our camping days were over.

The snow never stopped all day. All afternoon it came down harder and harder, until it became the biggest snowstorm of the past five years. Virtually everything was shut down, the radio and TV were broadcasting warnings to stay off the roads, and the interstate into the city was closed. We knew we weren't going to be able to make it to the hospital the next morning. And as it turned out the hospital was closed anyway. Nurses and doctors couldn't make it either. My doctor's office called and re-scheduled me for mid-April.

Mid-April. So now what were we going to do about listing our house? It might sell before we were ready. On the other hand, we knew it usually takes time to sell a house. Just because we loved ours, someone else might not. It wouldn't necessarily be snapped up by the first person who looked at it. And we had heard the market was slow just now. But if it *did* sell right away, I wasn't going to be able to do much, so soon after surgery. Yes, no, yes, no. Finally we decided yes, we would go ahead and list it effective the first of April. Might as well get started.

A dribble of lookers came through right away, then fell off. I began to think we were going to have trouble selling. Then, just five days after my surgery, our realtor called one mid-afternoon wanting to bring someone through in about an hour. "That's very short notice," I pointed out, and she agreed, but pressed the issue. "We're in the area now, looking at properties, and these people's house has already sold; they need to buy very soon." I said OK.

We had made it a practice always to leave and go grocery shopping or something while lookers were there. Realtors prefer it that way. Above all, they want to avoid any awkward encounters between buyer and seller, with questions, like "why do you want to sell?" If we had that one put to us, we had a perfectly sound reason, but it wouldn't do to let our misgivings about the unpaved road and other issues show through. It happened that Loren was gone for some reason and, having barely resumed driving, I didn't feel like cruising around very long. So after twenty minutes I chanced it that the lookers were gone, and headed home. When I pulled into the driveway, there was the real estate agent's car and her clients were standing there next to it. They had seen me. It was too late to back out and go on.

She introduced us. "Nice place," they said. "Love that water recovery system. And the nice lot next door. What's the little concrete slab on it for?"

I said I had no idea, that it had been there when we first saw the two lots and the people we bought the second lot from said it had been there when they first saw it themselves.

"Why are you wanting to sell?"

There it was, the dreaded question. The agent winced. But I didn't have to hesitate a beat. "We have a son in Texas," I said, "who needs us."

The offer came the next day—a good offer; we would be making enough profit, mainly on the vacant lot, to cover our moving costs with some to spare. But it called for possession in thirty days, a little before the end of May. There are times when a person doesn't know whether to be glad or sorry.

We accepted it, of course.

Moving on meant not only leaving the house and life we'd built there, but also the idea of permanence itself. We had spent our adult lives on the move and had come to New Mexico to build our last house. We had liked the prospect of never having to move again. Now, by selling, we were showing that we had given up that hope. Oh, there would be a last place, of course, there has to be, but we saw now that we could not know or choose what it was going to be. In leaving our house on the ridge, we were going back to letting "home" mean what it had meant before—a contingency, a day-to-day state of mind.

We had also let ourselves think retirement would mean freedom from constraints on our time and what we chose to do with it. How foolish! We don't, any of us, ever live entirely to ourselves; we are always constrained by pressures from without, or, for that matter, from within. Love itself is a constraint. If we choose to love, we can never be totally free agents.

We signed the papers, choosing to become transients again.

One afternoon as the time was getting close, I took a break from packing and went out to walk our trail around the perimeter of the property. As I was crossing a bare stretch toward the back, I suddenly realized that I was seeing another trail through the sparse grass. It was a very narrow one, only a few inches wide, that went at an angle to our own. It must have been there all along, unnoticed. But now that I *had* noticed it, it was obvious—and obviously a deer trail. To verify that, I left my wide trail and walked along beside the narrow one I had just found and, sure enough, saw deposits of pellets. We had known, of course, that deer frequented our lot, but I had imagined they passed through more or less at random, on impulse. Now, seeing this worn path they had made, I knew that they crossed in regular, habitual patterns of long standing. Once again I felt my own transience on those acres. They had been crossing them long before the noise of rock-breaking and compacting of soil and hammering began, and I could only suppose—hope—that they would still be crossing for a long time to come.

The deer path reminded me, too, that even though our patch of land looked so austere, so close to the very ribs of the earth, it was in fact quite vulnerable to wounding. The soil bruised easily. Even before we built our trail, the random strolls we took around our five acres had left the beginnings of paths. How long would it be after we were gone, I wondered, before those paths and the trail we had made with so much effort would heal away? I would have liked to believe that all traces of our presence would disappear, even the concrete foundation, and it would be just as it was before we came, beautiful and austere, with only the deer trails.

PART FOUR

Back in Texas

CHAPTER TEN

Building It Again

MOST PEOPLE WHO have been through the experience of building a house say "never again." It's easy to
understand why. Yet even while we were in the thick
of it, I knew I'd do it again in a minute.

Now we were not only going to build again, we were going to
build the same house again. I suppose that is something very few people ever get to do. You hear people say they wish they could live their
life over again and try to get it right—an option not available to any
of us, and it's probably just as well. But Loren and I did get to build
our house for retirement again and try to get it better.

One thing we had learned from the first try was that when you
build a house you're not going to get everything right. You just aren't.
In spite of all our careful planning, there were things we wished we
had done differently. The peak of the living room ceiling, for
instance, wasn't centered over the fireplace; the toilet in the guest
bathroom was in plain sight from the back end of the living room.
None of that kept us from enjoying our home and having a good life
there. But as long as we were doing it again, we thought we might as
well tweak it a little. So during the busy time between buying our lot
in Glen Rose, in January, and pulling out of the driveway with all our
possessions, at the end of May, we plunged into another round of
planning.

Three years had passed since our retirement. They had been
three very full and in some ways fairly troubled years, and we both
felt that we'd aged more than three years' worth. Our energy levels
had notably decreased. Even so, the pattern of how we lived our lives

and of how we wanted to live them had stayed pretty much the same. So our needs and wishes in a house were also basically the same. We wanted two spare bedrooms so family and friends could come visit. We still needed easy chairs in more than one room so if I wanted to watch a baseball game on TV, say, and Loren wanted to read, there would be comfortable places for both. And we still needed our own work areas—because we were both still working. We'd had these needs in mind from the start in planning the house, and it had accommodated them well.

There were just a few adjustments to make. The square shape of the living room had made it hard to arrange furniture in a conversational grouping—we made it a foot longer and a foot narrower. This meant making the kitchen a foot longer too. The entry hall had proven to be so shallow that opening the door and taking people's coats and getting them to the closet (behind the door) was awkward, so we made it six inches deeper. (It ended up not being enough.) The hall bathroom arrangement was put back more or less the way Loren had it in the first place, but a foot wider because we extended that whole side of the house by a foot. Even with all my arranging of cardboard models of furniture, I had failed to realize that there wasn't going to be enough space to get around the twin beds in the back bedroom comfortably when making them up. Living in a space beats looking at it on paper every time. So we fixed that. The breakfast room that we had already made a foot deeper than the purchased plans allowed grew by another foot, for more ease around the table. The peak of the living room ceiling was centered over the fireplace, and the double windows in our back bedroom wall were moved over a little to center them under the peak of that ceiling.

Most important of all, we widened several doors to make the house wheelchair accessible, just in case. Joyce, the builder's wife, had urged us to make the house wheelchair accessible the first time. We had resisted the idea then. But now, after only three years, we better understood that we couldn't know what was ahead. So we went to a medical supply store to measure a wheelchair, and I made a little cardboard model like the furniture models and "drove" it around the plans to see how it cornered.

Naturally, this second planning process wasn't nearly as hard as the first, since we basically knew what we wanted and the plans were still on Loren's computer. But making small changes still takes a lot of thought and involves a lot of work on the part of the person doing the computer graphics. He spent hours at the keyboard, translating our ideas into workable drawings. What emotions he felt as he did this—sadness, regret, resentment, maybe, at having to do all this work when he didn't want to leave anyway, grim determination—I can only guess. We were not talking a lot during those weeks. We muffled what we were feeling, knowing that to vent at this point would only disrupt the remaining days as we counted them down. But I have to think that as he worked on the plans he felt at least a touch of anticipation, excitement, a hope that it was going to be even better this time.

Doug's reaction to the news that we were building the same house again took us by surprise. "You can't take a house apart and put it back together again! It has to stay where it is!" He simply could not wrap his mind around it. Finally we put it to him this way: It was going to be just the same getting from the recliner chair to the eating area as it was in New Mexico, and it was going to be just the same getting from his bed to the bathroom and back. With that, he got the idea.

During that same period when we were tweaking the house plans we were also choosing a builder. I suppose we felt somewhat less daunted by the thought this time, but it still wasn't easy. Experience seemed to have given us only that, experience, not any greater understanding of how to make a good decision.

The legal closing on our lot was in February. We could have done it by mail and avoided another twelve hundred miles or so on the road, but we decided to go to Glen Rose for the closing and use that as an opportunity to meet with builders, show them our plans, and try to get a sense of how they went about their work. Our realtor helped set up appointments for us with four different builders.

Two we eliminated quickly. One had come down with the flu and had to send an office assistant in his place, and we weren't able to get any sense of him at all—or of his houses, since the assistant wasn't able to show us any. "He's mostly building around Weatherford these days," she said. That seemed like reason enough to mark him off the list. We didn't want a builder whose time would mainly be spent elsewhere. A second was dropped because we found him irritating. "Anyone who doesn't want to use wood windows instead of vinyl," he said, "I just don't want to work with." That struck us as a little prescriptive. We didn't care to work with him either.

Between the remaining two the choice wasn't so easy. We felt a lot of confidence in both of them. But we felt more comfortable with Steve, the frank-faced younger brother of a father-and-two-sons partnership. We hit it off with him, and in the end that was the basis on which we decided—that plus the way he presented his bid. The other builder seemed to figure his up on the back of an envelope; after studying our plans for a few days, he phoned us with a price, but seemed unable to break it down when we asked about specifics. We thought that might lead to misunderstandings later on. But Steve sent us a spreadsheet with the numbers clearly broken out so we could tell exactly what was what, in case we needed to cut back somewhere.

Another thing we liked about Steve right off was that, without being pushy, he was willing to make suggestions—and good ones. Why, for instance, were we calling for six-inch outer walls? He could understand that thicker walls (meaning thicker insulation) would be good for New Mexico's winters, but we weren't going to have winters like that in Texas, and we could cut costs by framing with the usual two-by-fours instead of two-by-sixes. But we reasoned that better insulation would also help with Texas summers. We kept our six-inch outer walls and thereby kept our nice deep windowsills, convenient resting places for a book or a Kleenex box, but we were glad he was trying to save us money. He also asked why we were calling for so many recessed, or can, lights. Because they left a sleek ceiling, we said, and reduced the number of light fixtures we had to choose. "But every one of those recessed lights means punching a hole in the insulation and losing energy-efficiency," he pointed out. Ah! Hadn't thought about that! We cut down on the number of can lights. "And about those skylights in the utility room and master bath," he said, "you lose heat up those big skylight shafts in winter and they transfer heat in from outside in summer." He suggested, instead, a kind of closed tube that would let in light but leave the ceiling intact. We thought that sounded good. And indeed our house holds its inside temperature quite well, winter and summer.

We had assumed all along that this house was going to cost us more than the first one, and we were going to have to dig into our savings for the difference. Of course, we were lucky to have savings to dig into, but it wasn't an unlimited amount and we were a little uneasy. One of the items of concern that we discussed with Steve was the one that had cost us so much more than we expected the first time around: cabinets. Our specifications again called for factory-made cabinets, not because we were pleased with the ones we had but basically because we didn't know what else to call for. Steve and his dad pounced on that idea the first day. They were used to doing custom-built cabinets, they said. Steve drove us to see a house they had under construction, and the cabinets did indeed look great, wonderful. OK, we said, work up the bid on the assumption that we would have carpenter-built cabinets. But we were still worried about the cost. If factory-made ones with their particle-board components had cost us fourteen thousand, and the tweaking of our plans had slightly increased the total number, and if the custom-built ones used all solid woods and plywood, no particle board, then this was going to run the price sky-high.

What a nice surprise, then, when the cabinet line on the spreadsheet showed just half of what we had paid before! And the total bid was almost exactly the same, even with a regionally appropriate limestone exterior instead of inexpensive stucco. We were greatly relieved.

Steve's bid had one remaining question mark, though. He couldn't figure the cost of the driveway and front walk until he knew exactly where the house was going to sit on the lot. The longer the driveway and front walk, the more concrete they would use. And until he knew where the house was going to be positioned he couldn't start the preparatory dirt work. So two weeks after my hand surgery and four weeks before we had to vacate the New Mexico house, we made one more quick trip to Glen Rose, to mark off the footprint of the house. Mostly, of course, it was Loren who tramped around and crawled around in weeds under the hot sun, measuring distances and angles and hammering in stakes. All I did was hold the end of the measuring tape. When we hit the road that evening, we were hot, tired, and dirty. But the worst was yet to come. In the motel that night we discovered that we were eaten up by chiggers.

I believe chiggers are mentioned in the old song "The Devil in Texas." If not, they ought to be. There is no insect bite so itchy as a chigger bite. We slathered ourselves with anti-itch lotion and got up during the night to slather on more. It was several days before we quit scratching.

It appeared that our new place was going to have a bug problem as bad, in its own way, as New Mexico's centipedes.

This time, we didn't even consider renting a truck and loading up our stuff ourselves; the passing of three-and-a-half years had put that beyond us. But we felt sure that we could at least do our own packing. When we got back from laying out the footprint of the new house, we went straight to the U-Haul store, bought boxes and packing paper, and got started. As we went, we set a few things aside for a garage sale. Loren kept trying to insist that I leave the packing to him, but I wasn't about to. I might still be in a brace, but I could pack dishes, glassware, cooking utensils, whatever, with left hand and right arm. And did a pretty good job, if I do say so myself.

When things came out of their boxes again, all we found broken was the stem of one wine glass.

On the next to last day of May, the movers came and loaded everything up. After they pulled out, we made one more pass through the house to do a last bit of cleaning before driving out the white gravel driveway after them. Our custom had been to exit using the side that went between the house and piñon tree we'd taken such pains to save during construction. It was convenient for pulling ahead after backing out of the garage, whereas the lane that went on the other side of the tree provided a good swing into the garage. As we took the outbound lane for the last time, the piñon tree stood there in its little circle of dry grass with its two guardian rocks, still healthy and vigorous. I waved it goodbye.

It was not a happy day. We had not yet gotten over—and still haven't—the grief of leaving the place that we had chosen for our retirement over all the other places we might have gone and the house into which we had put so much thought and planning and hope. Yet it helped to know that at the other end, a young man as nice as Steve was already at work preparing us another good house, on another piece of land with hills and brush, in another quiet place.

Once again we headed down I-40 and U. S. 287 caravan-style as we had three years and three-plus months before, but this time in the other direction. Loren pulled an open trailer behind the Forester; I drove the Camry with the pendulum clock that had belonged to Mother and Dad on the back seat. Once again Loren had printed off a map from the Internet so we could find a house we had rented sight unseen to live in during the construction period. Our realtor had put us onto it, and we found when we got there that it was an average place, not as weird as the first sight-unseen house but smaller. We arrived Memorial Day weekend. When the moving van came with

our furniture two days later, we warehoused all of it in the spare bedrooms and garage. We were squeezed pretty tight in the space left
over. There wasn't even room for Doug to come spend the night.

But we weren't at all miserable there. There was a nice crape
myrtle bush just outside the living room window, with a mockingbird
nest in it, and we could stand and watch them fly in and out of the
foliage feeding their little ones. It was a Texas kind of feeling to see
those familiar white wing flashes and hear their varied warblings. It
helped us focus our minds on the new house where ground had
already been broken.

When the dirt contractor came back to work after the holiday,
we told Steve we would like him to go ahead and put in the garden
patch we had asked for. There was already a wide path going down
the slope behind where the house would be. It was worn there by the
people we had bought the lots from, now our neighbors across the
street. They had enjoyed driving their grandchildren down in an
electric cart to look at the pond in back. Along their cart path,
maybe ten yards down the slope and behind a thicket of cedars and
other brush, there was a level spot that was also fairly clear. That was
the place we had chosen for the garden. So the dirt contractor
scraped it off, brought in railroad ties to enclose it, and filled in with
(supposedly) garden soil—not nearly as fine and fertile as the mix
Angus had brought us. That very week, while workmen were rough-
ing in plumbing up at the house site or setting up forms for the foundation, I planted our garden. It was a ridiculous time to be planting
anything in Texas, with the temperature about ninety-eight and not
a rain cloud in sight. But I knew we wouldn't start feeling at home
again until we had a garden, even if, between the heat and the
drought and the fire ants, we didn't get a thing out of it.

Building proved to be even more fun the second time than the
first. For one thing, we knew what to expect. Moreover, our temporary quarters were only a couple of miles away (nothing in Glen Rose
is far) so we could run over to see what was going on however often

we wanted to. We stayed even more closely involved than we did the first time.

Once again, we missed the pouring of the foundation. I don't remember why. But we did get to watch most of the framing. Not every bit; it was too hot to stay and watch all day. We would drive over in the morning, watch for a while, go back to our rental house and work at our computers (me in a corner of the living room, Loren back in the bedroom) until mid-afternoon, then go over and watch some more.

We thought the framing crew on the first house was interesting, but this crew was even more so. Strictly speaking, they weren't a framing crew at all, in the subcontracting sense. Steve's first choice crew for the framing had been signed on for another job, and when the second choice crew was also unavailable at the right time he decided to frame it himself: he, his conscientious brother Clint, and their master carpenter and cabinet-maker Ted. As a result, we probably have the best-framed house in Texas.

Steve is an extraordinarily tall young man—six feet seven or eight, I suppose—and it was truly impressive to drive up and see him standing full upright on the high beam of the roof. Impressive, but also scary. It was a twenty-foot drop down to the concrete slab.

In New Mexico we had heard of a builder who told his clients they could not come to the site and look around until the house was finished. We didn't see how he could make that stick; certainly we wouldn't have put up with it. We would have wondered how shoddy the workmanship was if he didn't want us to see it, and would have managed to be out there to check on it. Steve was quite the opposite. All the time he and the others were framing, Loren came by measuring things as they went, and they never seemed to mind. We had already told them that the front door of the first house wasn't centered at the entry because of careless measuring, so they weren't surprised when he paid close attention to this one, and quite cheerfully made an adjustment of three inches.

Steve, our builder, up top during framing.

We had already learned that you can't expect to get everything perfect. And sure enough, several months after we moved in we discovered that the framing of the three-angle breakfast room wall, with its deep windows overlooking the deck and the far rolling horizon, was slightly off. The pieces of wall between windows one and two and windows two and three are not uniform in width. Do we care? Not really. It's not nearly as noticeable as the off-center front door was in the other house, and the spacious view outside the window is what draws the eye.

As closely as we watched every step, I failed to keep track of dates this time the way I had before, and so I can't reconstruct when things happened. I suppose that shows that as much as we enjoyed building again, we weren't really as excited about it. We no longer regarded it as a unique experience. The basic steps were essentially the same; we had seen them before. Certainly the people were different. We would drive up in the morning and hear Ted's tape player blaring Creedence Clearwater Revival at a high enough volume to hear over his sawing and hammering, and we would know everything was going along fine. A couple of times we picked up Dairy Queen burgers (his preference) and sat with him under the shade tree in front for a quick lunch. Quick, because it seemed that he barely

Admiring the white stone and green roof.

stopped long enough to catch his breath before he was back at it. Ted liked to talk, but he liked working better.

We liked the electrician again this time too. Not that he bore even the slightest resemblance to Charlie, but he was interesting in his own way. We thought he would never get out to do a walk-through with us, but when he did we enjoyed watching his fast work. We liked how he made a mark on the bare concrete for every plug and every switch, placing them just where we wanted them. Charlie had ignored the electrical plan Loren had so carefully worked out and never asked us before he made changes; he just put switches and plugs wherever he took a notion.

Things came at us too fast to keep track of. I do remember how we delighted in watching the white stone mount up on the exterior and how we sorrowed when the corner jet tub proved to be oblong, not the oversized triangle our plans had called for. But we didn't insist that Steve suffer the loss of ordering another one, and now we're glad, because the big triangular one would have taken so much water to fill. We're not much into bathing together anymore anyway. We despaired when the shower door came without a towel bar, and we were told it couldn't be added because drilling would shatter the tempered glass. We felt like applauding when Ted put in the peeled cedar posts on the front porch—he knew exactly how to do it. It's great to watch people work when they know what they're doing.

All these details were just as entrancing as they had been the first time. And yet we maintained a kind of emotional distance. We enjoyed our home building, but we had learned to hold it lightly. We had learned—though we should have known it all along—that one never knows.

This second time around, the cabinets were again a standout experience, but in a positive way. Ted started out with a pile of maple boards and selected the ones with the fewest knots, as we had requested. (They would use the knotty ones on another upcoming job; some people prefer them that way.) We could drop by the workshop any time we wanted to see how Ted was coming along. At Steve's suggestion, we had gone to the home store and studied the doors on the factory-made cabinets and brought back a picture of the one we liked best. Wouldn't you know, Ted didn't have the right router to do that one? He wound up building three different miniature doors, trying to get as close as he could. He was expecting to build plain fronts for the drawers, and when we said we didn't want them that way, because there would be too many plain surfaces, we wanted them styled to match the doors, he was greatly puzzled. The fronts for the deep drawers were no problem, but there was no way, he said, to make recessed panels and borders in the shallow ones. He scratched his head over it for all of half an hour, then figured out how to do it.

When the cabinets were finished and installed, we began to see how fine the detail work truly was. Even the ends of cabinets had solid panels and trim matching the door fronts, as opposed to the factory-built ones, which were finished with something like vinyl sticky paper over particle board. The tops were finished with ornamental molding. We hadn't asked for any of these extras. Ted and Steve had just gone into it with a certain standard in mind for how cabinets ought to be done, and had done them accordingly. In much the same way, Clint, who had learned his cabinetry skills from Ted and was doing the trim carpentry on the house, made a nice little cornice above the front door, on the inside. That was just how he thought a front door frame ought to be finished off. He too had standards to maintain.

Toward the end, I found a moment to take Ted aside and ask him, as a secret, to make a little dresser-top box for rings and such out of some of the scraps of maple from our cabinets, for Loren's Christmas present. And of course he did, and of course it's neat as a whistle. We enjoy remembering Ted and the joy he took in his job, as much as we enjoy our beautiful hand-built cabinets.

Just once in our dealings with Steve did he let his high standards for his product lead him into being somewhat high-handed. When the stonemason was ready to build the hearth for the fireplace, Steve asked us how we wanted it done. Stone up to the bottom of the mantel, we said (we had already specified a heavy chunk of plain, polished cedar for the mantel itself); painted Sheetrock above. We could tell he wasn't pleased with that idea. "Don't you want the stone to go on up to the peak of the ceiling?" he prompted. The sloped ceiling did center nicely over the fireplace this time.

"No," we said, "just up to the bottom of the mantel. We like to keep things simple."

When we came back the next day, they were putting stone on up to the peak of the ceiling. Apparently he just couldn't bring himself to do it in a way he considered wrong. And now we're glad. That flight of rough, white limestone makes a striking visual center for the room—or one of two visual centers. The main one is the pair of wide, uncovered windows across the back wall, overlooking the deck and the far view. It draws all eyes.

I think it was about the middle of June when the foundation was poured, though without having kept a record I can't be entirely sure. It was a summer of practically no rain, allowing them to make fast progress. We moved in the last week in September. Once again I had a trip planned (to a conference) and if we waited until after I got back it would mean another month's rent. Besides, we were just so eager to get out of our cramped rental quarters that we rushed our builder at the end, hassling him to let us in. It was foolish of us; we should have been more patient. Unlike the first time, though, everything went smoothly. No problem, no inspections left undone or not passed, no light fixtures placed wrong and having to be moved, no Charlie stepping through the dining room ceiling. But that also means fewer stories.

The actual moving in was one of the best parts of building the same house a second time. Just as we had known, this time, how the furniture was going to fit without making cardboard models to test the arrangement, so also when I unpacked boxes I knew immediately where to put pans or dishes without that groping for the best arrangement that usually goes with moving into a house. The paint colors were pretty much the same too, with the same pictures on the walls in pretty much the same places and the same quilts on the beds. We were able to wrap familiarity around ourselves from the very first day.

Yet the new "last house" both is and isn't the same. From the outside, with its white limestone walls and green metal roof, it looks considerably different from our house in New Mexico. And it sits on the land differently. There, our house was perched above us, looming over the squat trees, as we approached up the steep, winding gravel road. Here, we come through a smallish, rustic sort of subdivision on a blacktopped road, crest a sharp hill, and look down at it, nestled straight ahead in a slight hollow. Where before we had cactus and bare ground and piñons, now we have a large front lawn of soft Bermuda grass that browns out in the June heat, with small strips of grass in back and on the sides between the house and the native brush that fills—rather densely—our three-and-a-third acres. Because of the hill in front and the absence of a single visible house clear to the horizon in back, we have a comparable sense of seclusion though in fact neighbors are considerably closer. Here, of

The finished product.

course, instead of open windows in summer, we have constant air conditioning. This is Texas after all.

Instead of the patio we have a deck, and we made the front porch deeper, so the rocking chairs wouldn't hit the wall of the house. Even if they did, they wouldn't chip the rock as they did the stucco. Also, since the porch sits flat on the ground, it doesn't need a railing and doesn't have steps like the first one. It's a nice porch, but we don't sit on it and read or talk as we did at Cerro Espinoso. The climate isn't conducive to porch sitting.

As for the deck, that was another of Ted's handiworks. Our plans just said deck, no specifics. When the house was about half done, Steve asked how big a deck we wanted. We didn't know. So we stood in the scraps and debris at the back of the house with Steve and Ted and Clint and eyeballed it. "Oh," I said, pointing and gesturing, "how about going out a little way from this corner and cutting over to that corner?"

"Don't you want a bench?" Ted asked.

Of course we did. We just hadn't thought of it.

With no more direction than that, he designed it in his head, told Steve how much material to order, and set to work. It turned out to be bigger than we imagined, but a fine deck. The grandchildren

Loren enjoying the deck.

use the two wide steps down to the ground for playing with action figures, just as they did the front steps at the New Mexico house. We sit on the bench or in our wrought iron rockers and read or just look out at the far horizon.

There are differences, but it's basically our same house again. If we haven't felt the joy and excitement we did with our first "last house," we have at any rate felt quite at home. We are once again living our quiet life in our own way—a way that might strike many people as odd or boring, but it's right for us. I'm beginning to think that as long as we could have this familiar rhythm to our days, we could feel at home pretty much anywhere. Yet the house itself, the physical container of our possessions and our days, does matter. It is the shape within which life forms its patterns, and to some extent actually shapes those patterns. Building a house isn't the same as building a life, but the two overlap each other in major, if shifting, ways.

Certainly building again by the same basic floor plan has made Doug's life easier. His spatial sense is none too good at best, but he gets around much more easily here than he would if we had built an entirely different house.

Doug enjoying another cold one, this time at the kitchen table.

The truth is, he has always been a little uneasy with the layout of the house. The problem is that the two guest bedrooms are on the opposite sides of the house from ours, so we're not nearby in the night. We bought a baby monitor (though we didn't tell him that's what it was) the first time he came to see us in New Mexico and demonstrated to him how we could hear him through it. But he could never seem to get the idea. We've told him over and over to call out loudly if he needs us, but he seems to have it so firmly in his head that he should keep quiet at night that he doesn't do it. Once, Rick and Tina were visiting us in New Mexico at the same time as Doug. They were sleeping in the front bedroom while he, as usual, slept in the back one (the twin bed room), and they found him up during the night in the living room, trying to find his way back to bed after going to the bathroom. And once since we moved here I woke up sensing something amiss and found him wandering in the kitchen. Even then, knowing he was lost, he hadn't made a sound.

Until recently, then, his visits were something of a worry. We knew he liked being here, and especially enjoyed his evening ritual of sitting on the deck to have his pre-dinner beer, but at the same time we knew he was a little anxious about the sleeping arrangements. But no more. We finally thought of a solution. Now when he comes for overnight visits we close the door of the front bedroom and put a couple of kitchen chairs in the wide opening between the living room and the little small hall that connects the two guest bedrooms, so if he comes out of the bathroom and fails to turn left, the chairs tell him which way to go.

Since we thought of the chair system, there's never been a problem again and he no longer seems uneasy. If he wakes up in the morning before we do, he gets dressed, moves one of the chairs out of the way, and finds the velvet love seat to sit and wait until we come start the coffee.

CHAPTER ELEVEN

At Home in the Limestone Hill Country

OHN GRAVES, in *Goodbye to a River*, calls this "hard-scrabble country." He ought to know; he lives here. And he's right, that's what it is. The soil is thin and rocky, the grass sparse, the brush mostly cedar. Not good country for farming. The earliest white settlers who stopped their wagons here during a sequence of wet years must have been dismayed indeed when normal times returned and they saw what it was really like. Twenty miles to either the east or the west the land is level and soft. But here on our rocky hills it's more interesting, just so you don't need to make a living from it.

Somervell County (the second-smallest county in Texas) sits on the tip end of a northward finger of the Hill Country. There is a certain irony, then, in the fact that we're here, since we considered and rejected the Texas Hill Country when we were first thinking about retirement and now here we are after all. Of course, what people usually refer to as the Hill Country is several hours' drive to the south, but we're in limestone hill country, nevertheless. We chose this place because it was only an hour or so from Doug's place in Fort Worth, but also because Glen Rose seemed like a nice little town and, as a bonus, the landscape reminded us a little of New Mexico.

I guess it's the rockiness of the soil, the dry look of the vegetation, the quiet, the distance of the horizon, the big sky. Cedars are never my favorite, but they do look a lot like our junipers on the Cerro Espinoso. No piñons here, of course; they grow only at a certain elevation, in a certain climate. Here I look out the window beyond my computer screen into a crape myrtle. Right now, as I write, it's in bloom and waving its branches in a strong wind. Humming-birds are visiting the blooms of the red yucca plant by the window, and a little tufted titmouse keeps flying into the crape myrtle. On beyond, just inside the pipe fence beside the driveway, there's a big rock that the earthmoving contractor was going to push off the drop-off in back when he was smoothing things over at the end, until we asked him to leave it where it was. It reminds me of the guardian rock Angus pushed up beside the piñon in our gravel driveway. And just as before, I see nothing but woods across the road, though I know there's a house hidden back in there.

We like the slow, quiet pace of Glen Rose. There's an open air produce market on the square in season and a pie shop that draws rave reviews. The Methodist church runs a thrift shop where I browse the racks for dollar skirts and quarter tops and keep an eye out for good jigsaw puzzles. We have two grocery stores and a senior citizens center where Loren and I could go play dominoes and eat lunch if we ever got around to it. There's a bluegrass festival in the summer for folks who don't mind the heat. True, there's not a lot of choice in the way of restaurants, but we do have a good barbecue place. Actually, there are two barbecue places, but nearly everyone agrees there's only one good one—though which one it is remains debatable.

These days the hills that never afforded good farming are doing well as tourist attractions. Droves of people come here to camp, wade the rocky-bottomed Paluxy River (the second shortest river in Texas), and canoe the nearby Brazos. They drive through Fossil Rim, our really fine animal park and endangered species breeding facility, or try to make out the dinosaur tracks at Dinosaur Valley State Park. They browse our junk shops and antique shops. Tourism has brought a measure of prosperity to Glen Rose. But the biggest employer in the county is the nuclear power plant. We joke that you can tell Glen

Rose residents by their radioactive glow. Tax dollars generated by the
plant in its early years improved the schools, built a nice little hospital, and renovated the fine old Somervell County Court House. If it's
not too hot or too cold out, we can walk down to the courthouse
square, nose into shops if we feel like it, walk on up the steep slope
to the post office, come down again to linger over lunch, then walk
back home, breathing hard on the pull up the hill.

We're happy to be here in the hardscrabble country of the brushy
limestone hills. Everyday life is easier than it was on our ridge in New
Mexico, and we can do things for Doug that we couldn't before. The
very first Sunday we were here, we got a call from his residence saying he'd had a choking episode and been taken to the emergency
room, and we were able to be with him in an hour. We take him for
some of his medical appointments and can usually combine those
trips with dinner at what he refers to as "our favorite steak place."
All in all, we're very much at home in this house we built for our
retirement. Once again we hope it will be our last house. But we
have learned not to count on it.

Glen Rose is the kind of town where, when people realize you're
a newcomer, they ask if you've found a church home yet. I didn't
particularly like being asked that question. It implied such certainty
that I *ought* to be looking for one if I hadn't found it yet—a premise
I do not necessarily accept. It put me on the spot. If I said "no" or
"not yet," I was letting myself in for a recruiting spiel. "No, and I
don't want one" would have let me in for considerably worse. At that
point I didn't honestly know if I wanted one or not. I was still grieving the loss of our church in Albuquerque. So I was always left stam-
mering.

It is a question, though, that touches on something real. As we
get older, the need to be at home in our lives in an ultimate as well

as an everyday sense becomes more and more pressing. I'm not talking here about a need to get right with God, in the trite old sense
that has motivated untold numbers of deathbed conversions. I don't
think of religion as a fire insurance policy. There's an essay by
Jonathan Edwards—the same Jonathan Edwards of "Sinners in the
Hands of an Angry God"—called "On the Nature of True Virtue."
I've remembered it, over the years since I first read it, as a kind of
guiding light. Instead of trying to scare people into heaven, the great
Puritan preacher and thinker argues here that virtue can be true, or
genuine, only if it is pursued solely for the love of virtue itself, without any motive of reward or punishment. It seems to me the same
can be said of churchgoing, that it can be authentic, in Edwards's
sense of the word "true," only if it is done for its own sake, not out
of fear or hope for the beyond, Whatever the reason, church does
provide a kind of home for many people nearing the end of life,
whether that means a return to a place inhabited in childhood or the
reaching of a new equilibrium.

For me, going back to church in my older years has been a kind
of homecoming in both senses, though not a return to the same religion as I was taught in my childhood. Loren and I both were rigor-
ously churched in our early lives, but in this respect as in others,
both of us have walked paths that have taken us very far from our
beginnings. We both revised our views as we went along. I switched
from the Southern Baptists of my childhood to the more restrained
and liturgical Presbyterians as soon as I went off to college. Loren
migrated to the socially conscious Disciples of Christ but was kind
enough when we married to join me among the Presbyterians. He
knew I was more rigid in more ways than he is, and it would be more
difficult for me to change. In the decade before we retired we
became entirely and contentedly unchurched. When we decided to
try church again, and returned to the Presbyterian fold, we both
were and were not coming home. We found at La Mesa Presbyterian
in Albuquerque that the liturgy and music and people kept us

anchored and at home in our lives, even if our theological views didn't always stay within official denominational bounds.

When we moved back to Texas, we knew La Mesa would be a hard act to follow. But we made the effort, and now we drive to a church in the nearby town of Cleburne where the pastor reliably, every Sunday, challenges us to think. We still miss the friends we made in New Mexico, but we have new church friends we care about and who seem to care about us. So now if anyone asked me whether we've found a church home, I could comfortably answer yes. But I am no more certain we've arrived at a final "place" in this respect than I am that we've arrived at our last house.

Once again Loren has made us a walking trail that winds around the perimeter of our land. The trail has a little up and down to it, though of course not nearly so much as the one we had before. Also, there are fewer cactus.

We have deer here too, and actually see them somewhat more often than we did in New Mexico. There's a bare area just beyond the driveway where we see so many hoofprints that we judge it to be their regular exit point from the lower, back part of the lot to our neighbors' feeder across the road. Mostly, if we do see deer, it's at dusk—but sometimes we'll see them in broad daylight, grazing their way around the house.

The day after Christmas, our second year here, when Laura and Angel's Elias and Celeste were trying out their new walky-talkies on the trail, they came onto a deer caught in the wire fence at the back of the lot. I've been told this is a common mishap as deer jump wire fences; as the front hooves go down, the back ones come up and get twisted between the strands. Trapped that way, they starve. Hunters sometimes come across their skeletons. But Celeste and Elias's deer was still very much alive. They used their walky-talkies to summon their dad, and he and Steven were able to bend the wire and maneuver the hoof free. The deer bounded away. Steven said it was the first time he had ever touched a deer or heard one make a sound—a kind of mooing or bellowing of distress. So our place generated a story for the family lore that day.

Besides deer, we have also seen foxes, raccoons, one possum, and one large snakeskin, shed at the edge of our deck. No actual snakes, though we're sure they're here. This is rattlesnake country. (We didn't think about that when we bought here.) It's also roadrunner country. When Rick visited not long after we moved in, he saw one outside the window and—thinking musically, as he always does—sang it the roadrunner cartoon theme. But he said it didn't go "beep-beep" in return.

Sometimes before I go to bed at night I walk out onto the deck to check out the night sky. It isn't quite as good as the sky we had in New Mexico; the lower humidity there let the stars shine through even brighter, but it's still very good. One moonlit night just as I started out the door I noticed a dark blob about the size of my fist moving across the deck toward the steps. It was a tarantula. I called Loren, but by the time he got to the window it was just going over the edge. We took a flashlight and went warily down the steps to look. There it sat, hunkered down in the grass, looking up at us with pinhead eyes. So we had another animal to add to our tally.

When I asked one of the neighbors if she knew we had tarantulas around here, she said when she was growing up here there used to be great congregations of them under the streetlights on the square. She added that I should be glad we had one hanging around; they keep down the insects. Someone else I know who has lived here a long time said her daughter used to pick up tarantulas and let them walk up one arm, across her shoulders, and down the other. Whoa, not me! On the other hand, I don't feel quite as negatively about the tarantula as I did about our New Mexico centipedes, just so they stay out of the house. So that seemed like a good swap.

Then we found a centipede in the house—the biggest one I'd ever seen.

There's a line in Walt Whitman's wonderful elegy for Abraham Lincoln "When Lilacs Last in the Dooryard Bloomed" that goes like this: "O what shall I hang on the chamber walls? And what shall the pictures be that I hang on the walls?" He is speaking of walls and the hanging of pictures, of course, as mental "pictures" to hang in the house of memory. And his language of walls and the hanging of pictures also speaks to the centrality of houses in our human experience, specifically in the formation of memories, and to our sense of at-home-ness in the world.

Following Whitman's cue, I want to think for a bit about the actual pictures we have hung on our actual walls—the framed images with which we surround our days and our remembering and imagining. Not all of these have achieved an emblematic status, like the "pictures" Whitman proceeds to name for his mental house of mourning. Some have. But even at their most basic level, as mere ornaments, the pictures that we—all of us—choose to have around us every day hold significance for our lives, even if we don't stop and consciously take them in every time we walk by. They indicate something about us. And too, like windows, they can shape our vision both of the outer world and of our own inner world.

Loren and I thought carefully before driving nails into the unspoiled walls of our new house. As our own parents aged, we had seen the walls of their houses become more and more cluttered with knick-knacks until there was hardly any clear space left. This was especially true with Loren's parents, who had so many adult children (ten, not to mention grandchildren and great-grandchildren) trying to figure out what to send on gift occasions. We wanted to avoid that kind of cluttering of the walls if we could. Yet many of our pictures had sentimental associations that made it seem a shame to leave them in a dark corner of a closet. We wound up hanging quite a few.

The first to be hung was a watercolor and ink drawing of a Shalako figure, one of those sacred in Zuni mythology as a messenger of the gods. This had been done for me by a student at Texas A&M, Chad Burkhardt, as a thank you gift for my having written recommendation letters for his law school applications. I found it in my department mailbox just before he graduated, along with a note. The next time I ran into Chad, I expressed my appreciation for such an elegantly done drawing and added, "I hadn't known you were an artist."

"Oh," he said, "I sell through a gallery in Dallas."

How perfectly that demonstrates the mysteries of the enterprise of teaching. We never know the fullness of our students' lives, rarely have even an inkling of how we may be touching them. I stop and look at this picture as I pass between kitchen and bedroom. It speaks to me of the cold December night Loren and I spent looking in windows at the Shalakos dancing, but also of many mysteries—of this student and his multiple abilities, of artistic capability itself, of teaching, of Zuni spirituality, of spirituality in whatever form.

On a short piece of wall between the kitchen and the Shalako drawing we hung a small oil we bought at our church's art auction the last summer we were in New Mexico. A dark impression of a mountain landscape, all smoky purples, it reminds us of that place and that fun event.

On beyond the Shalako picture, toward the bedroom, is a short hall branching off to the utility room. We chose that spot for a color copy of an advertising poster given to us by our friend Roy Alvarez. An ad for a grade-B Gene Autry movie may not sound worthy of framing and hanging, but this *Oh Susanna* poster is an item of great family importance. In small letters under the singing cowboy's smiling face are the words "with Smiley Burnett, the Light Crust Doughboys, and Champion." My dad is in it; he played fiddle with the Light Crust Doughboys. We have a tape of the movie and there he is, before I was even born, young and handsome and grinning as he fiddles.

In our bedroom we have two other pieces from the 2005 La Mesa Art Auction: an intense red semi-abstract oil suggestive of a ship under sail, painted by Robert Wirz, a friend of some friends of ours there in the East Mountains; and a pastel of mountains and mesas in wildly imaginative purple and green and orange, painted by Roger Beaumont, a fine historian who retired from Texas A&M a year after Loren and I did. I solicited the donation of both of these pieces for the auction and then bought them myself.

Also hanging against the dark green wall of our bedroom is a piece we bought in 1993, when we were at Auburn. It is a small, narrow watercolor landscape mounted in an intricate wooden box with doors and pediment, and I knew the minute I saw it in the faculty art show that it would have special meaning for us. Both my parents had died in the months preceding our move to Auburn, and Loren's mother died the spring we were there. The painting shows, in its top few inches, the world we know, with trees and sky, but has a great depth below where all abstract forms in brilliant colors surge and strive. It speaks to Loren and me of the power of life, the underlying vitality that sustains the surface we occupy during our brief lives and keeps it all going. Thanks, Ann Markle, for painting this.

In the living room, the expanse of white limestone that Steve had the stonemason lay on up the wall above our mantel makes a fine background for a Carol Grigg print of a Navajo woman on a horse. I bought this nice print years ago with money from a service award presented to me by the graduate student association at Rice when I left to go to Texas A&M. I've always liked its colors, the poise of the dignified rider as she gazes off into the distance, and the whimsical horse seeming to smile in smug satisfaction with its horse-ness. This piece was especially appropriate in New Mexico, but after all, we're still in the Southwest, and we brought along some New Mexican native pottery to keep it company.

On the wall opposite the hearth is a signed poster of a painting by John August Swanson called *Justice and Peace Shall Kiss*. Don't we hope! The words themselves appear below two emblematic embracing figures. Other words from Psalm 85 also incorporated into Swanson's scene of kindly agricultural folk are: "Justice shall look down from the heavens" in the sunbeams, "Truth shall spring out of the earth" in the roots of a tree, "Kindness and truth shall meet" above a pair of farmers in overalls shaking hands. Both words and picture offer consolation on days when the news is bad. "Justice and Peace, Truth and Justice," Loren said on one of those days. "Doesn't sound much like Shock and Awe, does it?"

Mr. Swanson sent us the *Justice and Peace Shall Kiss* poster as a gift when we bought one of the two fine serigraphs by him that hang in our dining room. In one, Jacob lies asleep on the ground while angels—splendid ones, among vivid stars in the night sky—come and go on a ladder. In the other, Jesus's baptism by John takes place while children play and have their baths in the river, women draw water, people work alongside the river in fields. Except for the descending dove and a ray of light, all these activities appear to be equally valued. The sacred is immersed in the everyday. Directly beside the baptism picture stands a deeply carved corner cabinet, made in Mexico. We bought it in Albuquerque. I think Mr. Swanson, whose mother was Mexican, would be pleased. In addition to the two serigraphs and the corner piece, the double window in the front wall is flanked by my mother and dad's chiming clock, with its steady pendulum, and the land patent for my great-grandfather's farm in Red River County, Texas, the farm where Mother was born and grew up, framed in dark wood. I found it folded up in Granny's shoebox of papers.

My little computer alcove behind folding doors off the dining room is the only space in the house whose walls are actually cluttered. I dislike clutter as much as I dislike noise (clutter of another kind). Nevertheless, my work space is not only cluttered with piles

of paper but with pictures I like to have around me as I work—my
diploma for my doctorate, on real sheepskin; a snapshot of Loren and
me with champagne glasses in hand at some festive occasion; a very
nice close-up of Loren in tux and black tie; a photograph of myself
carrying the university mace at the head of the faculty procession;
and a small water-color of a tall blue house in Valparaiso with the sea
in the background, bought from a street vendor beside that very
house.

In the guest bedroom wing, the short hall that runs between the
two bedrooms, past the bathroom door, holds three framed photographs that Loren took—a close-up of a dogwood blossom, a log
cabin in Smoky Mountain National Park, a path through woods. The
front bedroom has a poster of Georgia O'Keeffe's jimson weed painting, all blue and green with a single white flower. Its colors are
repeated in the Irish chain quilt on the bed. The back room is where
Loren has his windowed work area in the corner. On the wall beside
his desk is a print of Frederic Remington's melancholy painting of
cowboys closing a gate in the fenced-off range on a snowy winter day.
Loren spent his childhood on a ranch in Nebraska that was frigid and
snowy like that in winter. Beside the Remington hang his father's
worn spurs on a fine dark hook. Above one of the beds hangs a
poster of a terra cotta vase with two white blossoms against a misty
blue mountain background—a very common image. I had put it in
our garage sale when we left New Mexico, but it didn't sell, and when
I looked at it again I found that it washed me in tranquility. This
deserves wall space, I thought. Above the other bed is an equally
tranquil print of a single white blossom on a black field, in a gray mat
and frame. Rebekah, who does not have money to spare for non-
essentials, bought this for me for Christmas our first year here. She
explained that she had looked for something "classy"—like me. How
very nice!

"O what shall I hang on the chamber walls? And what shall the
pictures be that I hang on the walls?" These pictures on our walls are

for more than looking. Like our abundantly windowed house itself, they both define and open up our life here.

The periphery of our lives draws in ever more tightly to this quiet place as travel becomes more daunting, more tiring. We want to take another cruise, we want to go visit our children and grandchildren, but health problems keep popping up, and we find it hard to get ourselves onto an airplane. We enjoy being where we are. Loren always has muscle-taxing projects going on outside. That was one of the reasons he wanted to buy three lots rather than two, so he would have plenty of room for projects. He still toils through abstruse mathematical problems, while I still pore over literary texts and commentary and footnotes. So far that hasn't stopped. So I guess we haven't entirely found out yet who we are when we're not working.

And now a new element has been added that absorbs hours and hours every week and also holds us close to home, almost the way a job would.

It happened this way. We had been in Glen Rose only a couple of weeks when we very foolishly decided to walk from our rental house to the post office, on the other side of the main drag. The temperature was about 105°, but even so, we found crossing the highway so hair-raising that we decided to take the long way home in order to cross back at the town's one and only traffic light. From the post office, we went down the steep hill to the square, but before proceeding on our way past the courthouse and up the hill on the other side we popped into the air-conditioned Thrift Shop to cool off. Coming out (with a red linen dress under my arm that I'd bought for a dollar), we saw straight in front of us a sign saying Food Bank. We had both done a little work at the big Houston Food Bank long years before, so we knew what food banks were. We went right up, were given a tour, and said we wanted to volunteer. And we've been at it ever since, packing boxes and giving them out twice a week, helping unload and shelve truckloads of food once or twice a month. I'm now the manager, so I also place orders at the regional food bank—a warehouse more or less like the one we remembered from our Houston days—and submit monthly reports, keep a monthly record of the temperatures of our refrigerators and freezers, recruit volunteers, and put out a newsletter. Between the food bank and the other business of life—reading, writing, quilting—my days are very full.

Sometimes, when I read, I sit on the deck, but my favorite reading spot is the comfortable swivel rocker in our bedroom. I haven't yet hung my head over the arm to get an upside-down view, but it does remind me of that bedroom rocker long ago. I can look up from my book and have views out of the deep windows to my left, which overlook the deck and the expanse of green out to the horizon, or out the shorter windows directly in front of me, which look out directly into the crown of a good-sized tree rooted just beyond the drop-off. In winter, with cardinals in its bare branches, it's like a Christmas card. Sitting in one or another of these good reading places, or propped in bed before going to sleep at night, I've resumed my Dickens splurge with *David Copperfield* again and *Little Dorrit*, Anne Tyler's and John Irving's latest, and some biblical history and commentary, Harriet Doerr's two wonderful novels about Mexico again, and John Barry's *Rising Tide*, about the great flood of the Mississippi. So many books, so little time!

At the time we moved I didn't know if I would ever be able to quilt again. The thumb-wrist joint that had undergone reconstructive surgery still hurt, my hand had lost much of its flexibility, and various finger joints had arthritic bone spurs. It is a measure of my desperation that I actually resorted to the sewing machine to finish a quilt for Beka's Christmas present. I've never enjoyed quilting on the machine. I'm a hand quilter. So I worked hard on my therapy exercises and was soon able to do a little at a time, then more, until now I'm back to where I was, even though the hands still hurt. My favorite way to quilt is with a baseball game on TV in the background, and being back in Texas has meant getting Astros games more often, so I've quilted along with a good many of them—but not with Rangers games. I'm strictly a National League girl.

There are still days when the fingers hurt so much that I put away whatever I'm working on. I was lamenting this to Alan one day by email, saying I was once again fearful I was going to have to quit quilting before long, and he fired back a reply that he hoped I would make him one more "before I hung up my thimble." I told him to think about size and color.

His phrase about "hanging up my thimble" struck me as witty, so I passed it on to Rick. "Well, I want another quilt," he said. I told him to think about size and color. What he and Tina came up with, after weeks of thinking and sending pictures back and forth, was apparently based on Vivaldi's *Four Seasons*. They wanted four big bear paw blocks in different colors for the four seasons, with lots of white background for fancy quilting. But, as I said, it took them quite some time to think of this. In the meantime, Steven happened to phone one day while he was out walking the dog and I again shared Alan's thimble-hanging-up quip.

"I want one," he said.

I trotted out my standard line. "Be thinking about size and color."

"Queen size but not clear to the floor," he shot back. "About a twelve-inch drop. Dark blue and purple, with some pink and maybe just a little magenta."

So Steven's quilt moved from third in line to first, because he got his specifications in before the others. What I saw in my mind for the colors he had specified was a log cabin with magenta centers. It came out beautifully, though not quite as expected. The dark blue and purple that were supposed to predominate receded into the background and the pink stood out. I could tell when we unfolded it on his bed that he was just a little disappointed. So now I'm working on another for him.

Alan was still thinking. So Rick and Tina's came next. With large design elements and wide borders taking up so much of its total size, it went fast. And it turned out to be quite striking, even if somewhat odd. They may yet get another one.

By this point Alan had settled on a pattern and knew he wanted red and black on a neutral background. But what shade of red? I asked. "Like tomato soup made with milk." After standing in the fabric store for some time, trying to decide which fabric was most like that, I finally had to get samples for him to choose from. His colors worked beautifully together and were great to wrap myself in during baseball season.

Since then I've made quilts for Dan and Molly's three boys, a scrap tulip quilt that Alan's Caroline took home for her bedspread, a deep blue and green turtle quilt for Laura and Angel's Benjamin, a baby quilt for their new little Joaquin, and another bedspread for Loren and me, dusty roses and subdued greens in a flower wreath pattern, stunning against our green walls. I've bought fabric for a monochromatic cabin in the stars like one I saw at a shop in Colorado last year, all tans and beiges with big swoops of feathered garland quilting, and can hardly wait to get started, but I've promised one to Kenny's wife Shahla first. I want to make quilt after quilt as long as my hands can take it.

As I think about my sequence of quilts-to-be reaching off to the horizon, I look out at the intense blue of an early summer sky and see, once again, a lone buzzard soaring in the distance. To judge by the thudding noises I'm hearing, I'd say Loren is out moving rocks. He says he goes out to have fun. It's hard to believe. The fun's in here, with my needles and colors.

But I have other things to do this afternoon before I can settle into quilting. It's Friday, and I promised that before Sunday I would look through some materials for use as an adult Sunday school study guide. Thinking of church reminds me, I need to start thinking about a topic for the talk I promised to give for the women's luncheon. And for that matter, the talk I promised to give at the University of

Finishing another Irish chain.

Nebraska to celebrate the donation of a big collection of Willa Cather letters to the library. Cather family members will be there. This talk has to strike just the right balance. It looks so nice out, though, that what I'd like to do is go for a walk. Wish I could go down to the square, but better not take the time. Need to get started on a shopping list for Steven and Alexander's visit next week. We'll pick Doug up on the way back from the airport and bring him down for dinner. Wonder if he still resists spaghetti. How can anyone not like spaghetti? But maybe it had better be chicken the night he's here. Oh my gosh, I've got to get those article proofs read before I forget and have them after me again, wanting to know when I can finish them. Need to send Bob and Verena Wirz a note, hear they're both down now, one with a broken ankle and one with a hip waiting for replacement. Oh yes, want to go pick up a carton of cole-slaw from the barbecue place before it's time to start dinner. Wonder if we're going to be finished with Loren's annual physical on Monday in time to meet Paul at the Food Bank for unloading. He can't do it himself, too big an order. Anyway, he doesn't have a key, and . . . .

It's a good thing I'm retired. There wouldn't be time for a job these days.

One of the real rewards of coming back to Texas has been having cardinals around the bird feeder. Not that we didn't enjoy our birds in New Mexico, but we missed the cardinals. There are trade-offs in everything. We don't have piñon jays here, but we have mockingbirds. No Cassin's finches, but house finches and house wrens and Carolina chickadees, always a favorite. On January 17, 2006—the date is noted in my bird book—I spotted what I thought was an orchard oriole. And wonder of wonders, painted buntings have returned to the area after what I'm told was a long absence. In late winter we have lots of slate-colored juncos, handsome little guys with solid, dark gray backs and white bibs. I hadn't been acquainted with juncos until New Mexico; we had several varieties there. Didn't know there were any here at all. But according to the picture in the book, slate-colored juncos they are.

Vultures, or turkey buzzards, are almost as abundant here as the cardinals. Vultures are not usually regarded as an appealing bird, of course, but I've come to enjoy them as long as they don't gather in great numbers. One day we saw a whole convention of buzzards on a utility pylon at the edge of town, and so many of them together did look rather ominous. But I enjoy watching individual birds soar in the big expanse of sky above the bowl of green brush stretching away to the eastern horizon.

One day back in the spring I stood on the deck watching one circling, a single wide-winged vulture soaring and tilting in a wide sky. It circled lower and nearer, lower and nearer, until finally it was sailing past me just a few yards off the edge of the deck. At last it swept so close I could see its red head, its bright eye, the articulation of its splendid wing feathers, like long spread fingers. A handsome bird, in spite of its reputation. I half suspected its eye was on me, just as mine was on it. Each of us, to the other's eye, was firmly placed against its proper backdrop.

The buzzard soared on and away. I went down the two steps to the grass and on down to the garden, my eyes fixed now on the ground at my feet, instead of up toward the sky, to keep from tripping. Instead of an expanse, I now had a close view that shifted with each step—individual weeds, hoofprints, the loosened earth-crumbs of a fire-ant hill. Rocks in differing shapes were strewn along the bare slope: round ones like five-pound loaves that looked as if they could start rolling down the path without even a push, jagged triangles and trapezoids, round stones the size of tennis balls fit for lobbing at Goliath's forehead, flat limestone squares as level as stepping-stones, great boulders showing only a smoothed shoulder above the dirt. And something new among the rocks—dozens of three-quarter-inch toads, hopping every which way.

In the garden, I spent a few minutes admiring the new sprouts of beans that had pushed up through the crust since the day before. We had done our planting early this year, as one must in Texas, or else have everything burn up under the hot sun. Last year we had good crops of spinach, lettuce, and peas before the heat came on, but only the poorest, toughest green beans when summer came, and not a single tomato. We had counted too much on rain that didn't come. This year Loren tilled in a good infusion of mulch, what little compost we had accumulated, and some commercial fertilizer. By the first week in March, spinach and lettuce had popped up, little round faces of radish leaves were looking up at us from the ground, pea shoots were unfurling, and the first dark leaves of potatoes had emerged.

I did a little hoeing, then started back to the house and paused on the bottom step. The buzzard was still soaring, looking for dinner. It was too far away now for me to see its bright eye—the eye that had fixed on me momentarily and rejected me as not yet fit.

CHAPTER TWELVE

A Place to End

ONLY FIVE YEARS retired, and it seems a perfectly natural way to live. My days have fallen into a comfortable rhythm. Yet I know it is not a rhythm that will continue. The time will come—unless something unforeseen whisks me away first—when I will move into yet another phase of life, technically a continuation of the retirement phase but actually a different phase with a different rhythm marked by the presence of caregivers. Should we call that the post-retirement phase or the pre-death phase? As if I weren't in that phase, the pre-death phase, already! Of course, we are all in it from the moment we are born. *Media vita in morte sumus.* But it will be undeniable when I reach the post-retirement phase.

I wonder what I will look like as a very old woman. And will I still have an inner life? Will I still be attentive to the different shade of blue the sky takes on in October or the way a wren cocks its tail? Will I want to choose the dinner-time music to accord with the menu? Or will I not care? No one has told me what to expect. I saw my parents' aging and Loren's parents' aging, but that told me very little about my own.

Least of all do I know whether that final phase is still a long way off or fairly close. In just the five years since I retired I can see changes; the medical problems have become more frequent, the overall sense of well-being more fragile. So far, I don't fret about it. But I do see the world differently now that I am, as my brother recently pointed out, pushing seventy. I see things in people I never noticed when I was younger, never even imagined noticing. I see someone like Zbigniew Brzezinski, say, on television, someone I know is significantly older than I am (according to the Internet, born in 1928; I was born in 1939) and I think, "Look at him—old as he is, and he still has the energy to do all that! What an achievement! And what a mind! What a loss to the world it will be when he goes!" Such things never seemed so remarkable when I was young.

Human beings are said to be the only animals who know they will die. At what age I became aware that people die I can't remember precisely, but once I did, I don't recall ever having any illusions that I was going to be exempt from the general rule. It was when Loren and I began talking about retirement and giving so much thought to the building of our house that I began to think more about this and realized that in moving to what we expected to be our last house, we were moving to the house in which I hoped to die.

My point is, I'm content with that—with all of it. The reality is that I will probably die within the next decade or at most two. And that seems OK to me. Not that I would be comfortable with the specifics I would have to face if I were, say, diagnosed with some dreadful disease tomorrow and given six months to live. But in the absence of that kind of immediacy, I'm comfortable with the general idea. I'm comfortable with knowing that we at least tried to prepare the place where we would die. But I have even less confidence, this second time around, that it will work out that way. And the truth is, I'm not caring as much this time. I just hope to stay closely in touch with the realities of wherever I am, in whatever phase of life.

New Mexico was a particularly good place for becoming comfortable with the "real," especially those aspects of the real that might be thought harsh. It was a dry, hard land, all rocky and thorny, a land close to the geological skeleton, and for whatever time I had left I wanted to live very close to it indeed. When we left that beautiful, harsh place we may have been in some sense retreating from it, but if so it was because we were choosing to be more fully engaged with another kind of harsh reality that we knew we mustn't evade—

Doug's needs and limitations. I worry what his life will be like if he outlives us. It would be better if he did not. Not that his brothers would intentionally neglect him, but they have their own lives.

I don't worry, exactly, but do sometimes speculate about the order of Loren's and my own going. Unless we both go together, say, in a bad car wreck (just *crash* and both snuffed out at once), there will have to be some order—one first, the other second. Which, I wonder, would be worse? My first impulse is that I hope I can die first, because I don't believe I could bear to survive my dear, my darling. But I can't wish for him to have to endure the pain of grieving for me. So when I think of that, I have to hope to spare him by living longer. Clearly, there is no acceptable answer to this.

I suppose many couples who love each other think of these things.

At our place in New Mexico there was a spot up at the back of the lot, at its highest point, where the brush opened up and we could see for what seemed like a hundred miles back toward Texas. That was where I decided I wanted my ashes scattered.

I had thought about this matter of final disposition a few years before and had asked my sons how they felt about cremation, since what matters most is the feelings of those who are left. It was pretty clear they didn't want to talk about it. So I figured it was up to Loren and me to decide. After we retired, we had our wills reviewed for adequacy under New Mexico law and talked with the attorney about it. She said she could draw up notarized statements that we wanted to be cremated. But that left the question of disposal of ashes. If we were so fortunate as to be still living at home when we died, I said, I would like for the family to walk up to the back of the lot, toward the crest of the ridge, and dump my ashes out there, but Loren thought there were probably laws against that. So did she have any advice?

Her response was practical indeed. "Who would know? And besides, with the winds we have here in the East Mountains, you'll probably wind up back in Texas after all."

It occurred to me later that if Loren were still living there after I was gone, it might be best for them to wait, in case he would be bothered by walking on that part of the lot afterward. There's a line by Walt Whitman, in one of those poems where he rhapsodizes about the commonness of life and the joys of taking to the road, that goes something like "Look for me under the soles of your feet." But I didn't think Loren would really want to do that. And now that we are indeed back in Texas—both of us, and not wind-borne—the point has become moot. But the question itself remains.

When I've mentioned to him that I would like to think our ashes would be together, he has pointed out that it really won't make any difference since we won't know whether we're together or not. That's patently true. Still, I prefer to be able to think so now, prospectively. But where? His parents and several other members of the family are buried in a small country cemetery in Nebraska, called Lone Star, and he worries that whatever members of his family are left will think he has set himself apart or turned his back on the family in some way if he doesn't choose to be buried there. I could request Lone Star also and make things simple. It's a very pleasant place, with big cottonwood trees, nice and quiet. A friendly place, really. On Memorial Day people go out and decorate graves and sit in lawn chairs and visit. But then I think, how would my sons ever find it? I doubt that even Loren's could, unassisted. You go farther and farther from any main highway, up a series of narrower and narrower blacktops and then dirt roads, through the very dooryard of someone's ranch house, and down a wallowing sandy lane. But aside from the issue of whether they could find it—and why should they want to anyway? I don't visit my parents' graves—I also have the feeling I don't belong there.

Sometimes I think wishfully about the columbarium in the narthex of our church in Albuquerque. I don't know if our children would feel good about that option either, given that none of them lives there now that David and Angi have moved away. Still, we loved La Mesa, and we could be in adjacent boxes.

There's a lot I still want to do. I want to garden, as long as I'm able, and thrust my hand into the soil to find new potatoes on the leafy top-growth's root. I want to learn to recognize more kinds of birds without looking in the bird book. I want to listen to more music, and not just as background at dinner. I want to play more games of Scrabble® and win. I want to take Doug on at least one more train trip, and I want to take him somewhere outside the U. S. so he can use his new passport. I would like to see our grandchildren—all of them—graduate from high school, but since the youngest isn't a year old yet it seems doubtful. I want to make quilts that at last I'm completely pleased with. I want to send Heifer International enough money for a whole menagerie of animals every year. I want to go to park concerts. I want to see the food bank move into better quarters. I want to sit on the front porch on a fall day, after the first cool front has come through, and not think of things I need or even want to do inside.

There's a saying that has become popular in some circles—that the person who dies with the most marbles wins. What a stupid and shallow thing to say! Not that marbles don't matter. Of course they do. I wish every human being on this earth could have a sufficiency of marbles, instead of some having such an excess of marbles—whole boxes and bags and fistfuls of them—while others have so pitifully few. No, I don't dislike marbles, just the idea that collecting the most means winning. Certainly Loren and I won't have the most marbles when we go. On the other hand, we have collected quite a few. We both started in much less prosperous circumstances than we seem to be finishing in. We've been places neither of us ever expected to go. We live in a more beautiful home than either of us ever expected to enjoy. We were able, just this year, to pay for having Doug's teeth crowned—all of them. (He has a grinding problem when he sleeps.) We felt that would improve his life long-term more than anything else we could think of doing for him.

We don't quite know how this has happened. Somehow we've just always wanted slightly less than we could afford. The marbles we have—the possessions, the comforts, the treasures—are ones we very much enjoy. If the winners are not the ones with the most marbles, and I'm quite sure they aren't, then are they maybe the ones who most enjoy the marbles they have?

Among the trips that we never imagined we would be able to take was the Baltic cruise we took the year after we moved to New Mexico. We went to Copenhagen, Tallinn, St. Petersburg, Helsinki, Stockholm—wonderful, beautiful cities. But the place we liked best was Visby, Sweden, a small and very old town on Gotland Island.

Probably the most notable features of Visby are its intact town wall and its many ruins of eleventh- and twelfth-century churches. When we were looking at one of these splendid, broken, ivied old ruins, I was moved to quote Shakespeare's "bare, ruined choirs where late the sweet birds sang." Now, I don't usually go around quoting Shakespeare. Usually I don't even remember enough Shakespeare to quote him if I wanted to. This was an unusual moment, then, and Loren was understandably surprised. Equally understandably, he didn't know the source. So I provided it—the sonnet that begins,

> *That time of life thou mayst in me behold*
> *When yellow leaves, or none, or few, do hang*
> *Upon those boughs which shake against the cold,*
> *Bare ruin'd choirs where late the sweet birds sang.*

Later, back on the ship, I tried to think through the rest of the sonnet. No use, I couldn't call it to mind. But I did remember the final couplet:

This thou perceivest, which makes thy love more strong
To love that well which thou must leave ere long.

Shakespeare was speaking of himself here, exhorting his younger beloved to love him well because he, Shakespeare, would die ere long. At least, that was what he was doing on the surface—posturing, maybe, in a melodramatic kind of way. The sonnet itself is theatrical. But I think he had a more general and more important meaning in mind as well. I think he was saying to us, all of us, love *life* well because we are inevitably going to leave it ere long.

I don't mean to be morbid or plaintive here. I expect to have a long retirement. But experience tells me that the years will go by awfully fast, assuming I'm able to stay interested in the world around me. Our lifespans are only a blink. Even the youngest among us— even those who haven't so much as started to think about retiring— could say they will leave this world ere long. The point is to love it well.

Loren and I do love our life in this second last house we built for our retirement years. We like the lay of the land and this quiet little town and the barbecue place where the owner gives me a hug and asks if the beef and the okra were good. I like my hair cutter who calls me Baby Girl. Our second home for retirement may not have the sense of adventure that our first did, but it's more comfortable, homier. Life goes at a gentle pace.

Even so, a place you love to be is not necessarily the same as the place you fell in love with. I think about that spot up on the ridge at Cerro Espinoso where, for a while, I thought I would want my ashes scattered. I have not found such a spot here, on these acres. And even though this place (this house, our life in it) feels very right for us, that doesn't mean I can't imagine myself somewhere else. I hold it rather lightly, I suppose. That is something else that Cerro Espinoso taught us about retirement. If we had to pick up and move again—and who knows, we might—I think we would be able to go without the grief we felt when we left our first last house.

ISBN 978-0-87565-408-9

This Last House: A Retirement Memoir
ISBN 978-0-87565-408-9
Paper. $18.95.

LaVergne, TN USA
30 July 2010
191529LV00006B/204/P